LANDLORDOM
The Land of Jekyll and Hyde

LANDLORDOM
The Land of Jekyll and Hyde

How to be a successful landlord, anyway

Christine Dorothy

To order additional copies of this book, contact:
Xlibris Corporation
1-888-795-4274
www.Xlibris.com
Orders@Xlibris.com
121891

CONTENTS

- Could (or should) I actually BE a landlord?

- How do I start?

- Where do I get the money?

- What property should I buy?

- What are my responsibilities to my tenant?

- What if I breech the lease or the law?

- How do I find a good tenant?

- How do I get rid of a bad tenant?

- Is it a wise financial decision?

Christine Dorothy will show you if 'landlordom' is really for you and, if so, how to do it $ucce$$fully.

DEDICATION

Dedicated to my son, Brandon, who will be a landlord, willing or not, when he inherits my properties and to my sister, Susan, who is always there in the wings, enlightening me on the sour notes of having tenants.

CARD OF THANKS

Many warm thankyous to my Possel-Q, Pierre, who has kept me grounded and focused so that I could begin and complete this manuscript.

I'd also like to express my appreciation to my sister, Susan, whose stories contribute enormously to the Jekyll and Hyde-ness of 'landordom'.

It was a really attractive bungalow, a bit small, but the flower boxes punctuating the window sills and the dripping willows framing the drive way gave it instant curb appeal and I fell in love with it in spite of myself. The price was right and the time seemed nigh. The brilliant idea struck me to buy the place and rent it out. But, I tremoriously asked myself, "Would I actually dare to be a landlord?"

The condo was bright and spacious. The owner was selling privately and the price was tempting me. Would this be a sound investment over the long term with all the expenses including condo fees? Is making the plunge to be a landlord a wise decision?

INTRODUCTION

Rental properties can increase equity and provide extra income; at least this is the dream on paper. Some landowners are lucky and the dream unfolds as it should. Others, however, are not so blessed and the experience becomes a nightmare. On the up side, owning properties for rental purposes has great potential for monetary gain, but on the down side it has many pitfalls, one being bad tenants. It is an unforgiving fact that the poor behavior of tenants has given renting out property a bad name and has provided a good reason for investors to shy away from being landlords.

There are many laws in place to protect tenants that can seem to be unfairly stacked against the landlord. An uninformed and unsuspecting landlord can be tarred and feathered by a wily tenant.

Tenants are entitled, amongst other things, to hot and cold running water. Having to state this in law is on the level of an airline hostess telling you how to do up a seat belt, but its there, in the law. I never had to go out of my way to accommodate this requirement. If the law has to state this, you can only imagine what other hairline requirements there are. It's to your advantage to be aware of them.

Even though there is a heavy onus on landlords, the idea remains seductive to the young investor as he or she is lured by the prospects of additional income for their retirement, a time when the property would be clear of a mortgage and the extra income would add to one's projected comfortable retirement life style.

So you are thinking of succumbing to the temptation of 'landlordom'? Be aware that, early in the planning stages, before you've even purchased a place, you are entering into a fear-ridden arena in which you will either be eaten up by the lions of intimidation or you will come out victorious, having kept your verve to continue your shaky adventure into the rental world of tenants, leases, loans and repairs.

You can be assured that when you announce that you are contemplating becoming a landlord to friends and relatives alike, they will respond with the typical, 'Why would you want to do THAT?" Or, "Oh no, you don't want to have to deal with tenants. They'll wreck the place and you'll be stuck paying all the repairs." Unfortunately, this can be true as told again and again in one horror story after another by victim landlords.

The idea is to avoid these pitfalls by being prepared with good tenants, a solid, mutually advantageous lease, a good knowledge not only of the law but also of that seemingly nefarious institution, *'The Landlord and Tenant Board'*, in order that the plan will play itself out as in the dream and not in the nightmare.

Finding the right tenant is a key element in successful renting, but it is not all. There are many other aspects to consider before you leap. Do you have the type of personality to handle tenants? Are you solvent enough to get the money to purchase a place and then carry it in dry times? How do you motivate a renter to take care of your place? How do you get in to check the state of the residence to ensure it is being maintained, for example, that the cat is not using the apartment as a kitty litter box or that the renters are not using 50 extension wires in one power bar? Who pays for what utilities and when? How are you going to ensure the rent cheques are in? Who cuts the grass and who is responsible for snow removal? What about parking, noise levels and bylaws? Are there any things left on the premises that have to be accounted or cared for? Are you familiar with the laws of the Province or State, and bylaws of your Municipality?

And, you will want to consider how to get them out if they are high risk due to poor financial status (not paying the rent) or because they have a questionable (illegal) lifestyle. You leave nothing to chance when it comes to dealing with tenants. Many of these concerns can be covered in writing in the lease.

As the title implies, being a landlord can offer schizophrenic experiences. You think everything is going great (the 'Jekyll' side of things) and the most unexpected thing happens to blindside you (the 'Hyde' part). And the opposite is true. You find yourself in some hell hole not knowing how circumstances could get worse, and bingo, everything falls into place and you're on your way again.

Nevertheless, even though there can be hard times and set backs, here I sit at the dining room table at my cottage, looking out the window at the lake, writing this book and able to do so because of my tidy little income from my rental properties.

I want to share my experiences with you to help you succeed by avoiding pitfalls that I have encountered or heard about. But, this is not a legal document and it is not meant to cover all the legal aspects of renting in your area. It is up to the reader to familiarize him or her self further with the Provincial laws (or State laws if you are in the US) and local bylaws. Not understanding them is not an excuse for not abiding by them. One is subject to them anyway.

Let us assume, then, if you have read this far, that you have made, or at least are considering making, the tenuous decision of becoming a landlord and want to learn the basics of how to do this while making as few mistakes as possible. Well, continue on, then, and let *Landlordom, The Land of Jekyll and Hyde', How to be a successful landlord, anyway,* help you decide.

Herein, the term 'he' or 'him' refers to all tenants, male, female or to a group of more than one.

CHAPTER ONE

Deciding to be a Landlord:
Have you got what it takes?

Do you have what it takes to be a landlord? Be warned, it is not for the thin-skinned or feeble-minded, nor is it for bullies. Being a pushy, bossy, confrontational landlord is just as bad as being weak-kneed. Your life will not be enhanced if you are always on a negative curve with your tenants. You want this experience to enrich your life and not send you to the loony bin from stress.

You need to possess certain qualities just to survive psychologically, such as the ability to resolve issues with as little conflict as possible. It helps if you can deal firmly but kindly with people and not be easily intimidated by their tempers or illogical opinions. I had a tenant who refused to get tenant insurance, which was a stipulation in the lease, so it was grounds for eviction. I was satisfied to have him sign an agreement with me that he was solely responsible for his belongings and that seemed to ameliorate that situation, although I wouldn't recommend others do this, but on occasion, flexibility will triumph conflict.

Confrontations should be avoided. You need to be able to avert arguments, be strong enough to maintain your ground on tenant-landlord issues and have enough compassion to see their side of things to resolve the issue. I had a tenant who wanted to paint the apartment an obscure color. At first I was rather stunned at the suggestion and my answer was no. After thinking about it for a while, I thought, well, why not? It's only paint and can be redone when they leave. So I went along with it, mainly because they were long-term tenants and this was their home so they should be happy with it, within reason.

When a dispute has a solution in the law, call in the bylaw officer and keep yourself out of it as much as possible. For example, I had a tenant who was furious about the neighbor's dogs barking and began threatening her and her dogs. I called the bylaw office and they sent an officer over to have a little conversation with him. They also talked to the neighbor and the situation got resolved without my involvement.

You also need a certain objectivity so you don't get embroiled in the tenant's personal problems. It's not your concern if they are having a hard time at work or if they aren't getting along with their girlfriend. Your concern is getting the rent and making sure your property is being reasonably cared for.

Last but not least, you need the financial wherewithal to withstand dry times so that you don't lay awake at night in fear of financial ruin. Expect there will be times when the rent money won't be coming in and be prepared to cover expenses in the short term.

If you agree that you have all, or at least some of these qualities, let's move on to other basic requirements needed for 'landlordom'.

CHAPTER TWO

MoneyMoneyMoney

Money, being fundamental to just about everything from decisions in government to personal relationships, is a determining factor in your choice to become a rental property owner. You need money for a down payment and you need to be bringing in a regular income.

Money can come in the form of savings in the bank, investments, your home or other properties or assets you own. For the down payment, you can use liquid cash or borrow against these existing assets. You'll need to talk to your bank manager about what would be the best way, as there may be a few options available to you.

Once the down payment is covered, the property you are buying becomes the collateral for the loan. If you don't make the loan payments, the bank then owns your property. Remember, the rental income should be enough to cover all monthly essential costs with some left over. Essential costs include the loan and interest, utilities if applicable, taxes: property, school, water/sewer, insurance and the occasional unexpected expense.

If you have allowed for the unforeseen, you will have the money set aside to pay for a new furnace if the old one breaks down and carry the loan in times when the place isn't rented. This back up plan is essential to protect your investment.

Mortgage vs Line of Credit

Mortgages can be amortized for up to 25 years. If you do the math and calculate how much interest you are paying over that time, you will see that it will be about a quarter of the purchase price. For example, a $300,000 property may end up costing just under $400,000 after the 25 years. There is usually a penalty if you break the mortgage or sell the property. The bank wants their interest and will penalize you if you don't hold the mortgage for the term you have agreed on.

This is why I prefer a line of credit (LOC). A homeowner's line of credit is a loan against the property. Initially you need to come up with more cash for a line of credit than you do for a mortgage. Some banks require about 35% of the value of the home if the property is for rental purposes and not for personal habitation. Some banks have stopped giving lines of credit for rentals. However, if you can procure a LOC, I would recommend it is the way to go. Interest rates may fluctuate, but they don't fluctuate very much, and to keep your credit rating in good standing, you only have to pay the interest each month (which is tax deductible). This helps when you are having a tight financial period.

Advantageously, you may pay lump sums to reduce the LOC without a penalty and you may carry the LOC paying just the interest indefinitely. When you sell the property and stop the LOC, there is only a small fee to pay (around $200.00). I have paid properties off in less than 10 years using a line of credit. It is my experience that the cost of a LOC is less than the cost of carrying a mortgage.

The other advantage is, that once you have paid down your line of credit, you can easily borrow against it to carry the place when necessary. For example, if you put all the gross rental income into the LOC every month for 2 years, you could possibly have reduced your LOC by about $10,000. This means you can re-borrow up to that amount to pay for essential expenses, such as taxes or insurance, when the place is vacant and no rent money is coming in. If you own the property long term, you can ask the bank to reassess its market value and increase your line of credit. So, if they allowed you a $200,000 loan to start with and your property has increased in value, they could increase the LOC accordingly. Banks never give a LOC equal to the value of your house but it would be at about 60-70% of the assessed value.

For example, your LOC could go up another $20,000 to $220,000. Now you have $20,000 more borrowing power. The idea is not to use it, but to gain added security in case of an emergency. The goal is to pay the LOC off as soon as possible. Even when it is all paid off, you still have $220,000 borrowing capacity. You can use this credit to buy another property or keep it for security. Either way, it is a great backup to have.

Be aware that the banks will normally try to sell you their product: a mortgage, but, in my opinion, it is in their best interest as a business, not in yours as a consumer. A LOC may still be your best choice to finance a property.

Getting the loan

The first time you go to the bank, it would be to discuss if you even qualify for a loan. You will want to examine what options are available to you, such as a mortgage or a line of credit, and how much you can borrow. It pays to look around at different institutions to find the one that best meets your needs.

When you have established your borrowing power, you will have a good idea of approximately how much you can pay for a property and you are now in a good position to begin looking for a place.

Once you find your rental property, you will have to get back to the bank or mortgage company to apply for a loan and set up a repayment plan. Here is some information you will need to prepare for your application.

* Social Insurance Number
* Address and previous address if current address is less than 3 years
* Employer: address, telephone number, and previous employer information if current employer is less than 3 years
* Source of income, verified by pay stubs or bank statements
* If self employed, you will need the last 2 years Notice of Assessment from your tax return
* List of assets (car, home, investments, etc.) and liabilities (mortgage, loans, expenses)
* Mortgage statements and value of your home, if you have one
* Credit card statements

Payments usually begin up to 30 days after the closing date, that being the date the property is handed over to you as the new owner.

CHAPTER THREE

Your Rental Property: House or Condominium?

A house or a condo, what will it be? I have owned both and realize there are advantages and disadvantages inherent in each one. It depends on your risk tolerance level as to which way you want to go. In my opinion, I would say a house holds more risks than a condo, but more money can be made.

The Bungalow

When I look for a house, I look for a bungalow not a two-story house. The market value of a bungalow seems to increase in value proportionately more than a two-story home. I compare it to cars. When the smaller cars hit the market, the big cars dropped in demand because the smaller cars were more economical. With the increase in demand for smaller cars, the price also went up.

Right now in the housing market, we have people downsizing for the same reason: economy. Also, the demographic force of the baby boomers, who are reaching retirement and looking for a home without stairs, has made that small, inconspicuous, humble bungalow a hot item. And, for the landlord, the bungalow holds much promise.

The first thing I do when I buy a bungalow is to make two apartments, one upstairs, and one downstairs. In order to do this, I, previously, had to review the bylaws and make sure it was legal. If the Municipality had outlawed 'granny suites', I made sure there was an area in the house that is shared. This could be a kitchen, a bathroom, a common entrance or the laundry area. Having this shared area puts me outside of the 'granny suite' or 'separate apartment' jurisdiction because the *'Residential Tenancy Act' [Exemptions 5 (i)]* does not apply if there is a shared area used by both the owner (or his family) and the renter. Make sure this is clear in the lease that part of the home is shared. This is the way to conform to the no 'granny suites' bylaw, as the home is then not regarded as two apartments, but, rather, a shared lodging.

Getting around this legality was more of a problem before 2011, at which point The Government of Ontario passed a law, Bill 140, allowing basement apartments. The lack of low cost housing and the high demand for places to live by the lower income sector precipitated this legislation.

Individual Municipalities made their own guidelines to follow for this Bill. It's important to check them out.

Some areas require the basement apartment has two exits, to comply with fire safety regulations, to be legal. Many bungalows have an entrance from the basement to the garage and one from downstairs to the upstairs kitchen with a landing leading to an outside door to the back yard. This back door is used as the entrance for the downstairs apartment with the kitchen door being secured for the upstairs tenants.

The lower level apartment needs a bathroom and a kitchen. The bathroom could consist of a sink, toilet and shower. The kitchen needs cupboards, a counter, water (a sink), a fridge and a microwave, passing as a 'wet bar' and not as a kitchen. Eliminating a stove in the basement makes it less like a formal kitchen and therefore less like a 'granny suite'. This avoids provoking any existing anti-'granny suite' bylaws. But, if the Municipality is respecting Bill 140, and, thereby accepting the legality of a separate basement living area, then a stove wouldn't be a problem.

When I lived in the basement apartment of the first bungalow I owned, I did so without the use of a stove. I had a convection microwave, which acted as an oven, and I used an electric frying pan that did everything from roasts to soup, so I did not miss a stove. I would rent the apartment out to someone who was happy with this arrangement. After Bill 140, this became less of an issue, but something to keep in mind if your Municipality bans granny suites.

If an apartment or 'granny suite' is considered a 'non-conforming' apartment, it does not mean it is 'illegal'. It just means that it was preexisting before 1996 when Bill 120 outlawed separate, or basement, apartments. 'Non-conforming' also means that the independent living space was not registered as an apartment with the city, did not have a permit to build and, also, may not have followed the requirements for building and fire codes. Many Municipalities turned a blind eye unless problems arose. It was always a risky situation to rent it out as a separate unit. Risky because a dissatisfied tenant could report it to the Municipality and that could result in your not being allowed to rent it out. So if you are living in the house and are renting out a separate, independent unit, it is better to have one area that is shared.

Before you purchase a place for rental purposes, be sure to check out if you need to get a permit to do so. If so, you may be required to legally show it is up to safety codes.

To start off as a landlord, I would recommend you share your house with your tenant. This keeps you from having to renovate your place to be up to code for building and safety. Since it is a residence, it is likely not required to have the same building and safety codes as an official duplex, and you don't fall under the jurisdiction of '*The Residential Tenancies Act*'. Not only can you can circumvent a lot of the tenancy laws, but also this slow initiation allows you to learn about the rental market and helps you decide if you want to invest further in rental properties.

Living in the house with a tenant can trigger some security and privacy issues. One little trick I discovered was to have door handle locks installed on all the bedroom and living room doors. These locks were adjusted to match the entrance door. So the tenant only needed one key. I liked this idea for myself as it gave me extra security and I thought my tenants would like it too. So the downstairs keys were made to match the back door entrance and the upstairs room locks were adjusted to match the front door. This was especially important since the laundry was a shared area.

The first bungalow I purchased had a finished basement but no kitchen and no bathroom. I put out about $10,000 to $15,000 to install a bathroom and a bar-kitchen. I put the kitchen at the end wall of the recreation/living room. It wasn't as expensive as I had anticipated. If you are allowing for a stove, extra electrical connections have to be put in. All plugs and electrical outlets have to be by code, especially in the kitchen where GFI plugs are necessary. 'Ground fault interrupters' protect from electrical shock and protect against over use. This is essential for safety and for insurance purposes.

The bathroom cost a bit more than the kitchen, but if the plumbing is pre-existing in the basement floor, it isn't overwhelmingly costly to put in a three-piece bathroom. Everything has to be done properly because if something can go wrong, it will, so prevent potential problems by doing things right in the first place.

I feel that going the cheapest route is false economy. Quality is important and I never had the mindset that, if the place was to be rented or sold, to do it as cheaply as possible. Some money has to be spent to ensure a certain level of quality. I like to prepare and or repair things as if it were for myself. Spending a bit more ensures things will last longer and it saves money in the long run. Also, you want to do everything possible to protect your tenant from hazards. Doing things properly also ensures the insurance will cover you should a disaster occur.

Once there is a bathroom, a kitchen, at least one bedroom, and a living area for the lower level apartment, the place is rentable.

Let's have a look how you pay off the property. Take an example of a house that costs $350,000 and the loan is $300,000. Monthly income from the two apartments could be $2,000. Taxes and insurance may be around $400 a month, so the gross income would be $1600.00, taking off any utilities and repairs that you need to pay. If you put this entire balance towards your $300,000 line of credit, you will likely be able pay it off within 20 years, and that means you paid it all with rent money. If you get any windfalls in the process, you can put them towards the loan (without penalty on a LOC) and reduce the repayment time.

Every cent you put into the property is a tax deduction. The rent pays for improving your property and, as your equity is increasing, your taxable income is decreasing due to expenses you can claim.

Don't forget, along the way you can have the bank come and reassess your home, increase your line of credit and therefore, your borrowing power. That leaves you with more financial security and peace of mind for your investment.

I would always examine the property and do whatever necessary to make it safe. One bungalow I had, had a fireplace upstairs in the living room and one down in the basement recreation room. I converted these to gas fireplaces. It cost $4,000 for both of them, but it was worth it for me, not to be worried about the hazards involved in wood burning. They improved the property and the cost was tax deductible.

The other option for a bungalow is to rent it out to one renter. You would get less than renting out two apartments, but your worries would be less too. If you decide to go this route, do the math and ensure that all payments can be made with some extra funds left over for a slush fund.

As I previously mentioned, I lived in the basement of the first bungalow I purchased. I rented the upstairs, which was easier to rent and I lived downstairs. I thought it would be a hardship, but in fact I quite enjoyed it. It was quiet and private and I couldn't hear the traffic, the airplanes or the neighbors. Living in the property allowed me to get into the rental market while supporting myself and at the same time to learn the ropes of being a landlord. I was paying off my line of credit with the rent money and with as much of my income as I could.

Once I had reduced my LOC, I had the bank come back and increase it based on the increase in market value of the house over the two-year period since I bought it. I then was ready to rent out my own apartment where I was living and move on and buy another house using the equity I had accumulated in my line of credit. This is how I built up my rental properties. The rent of the two apartments paid off the line of credit on that bungalow. All along, the improvements I made were paid for with the rent money and were tax deductible. I did the same thing with the new bungalow. I made two apartments, this time living upstairs and renting the lower level. As the line of credit was paid down, I was able to increase it with each reassessment by the bank and, with the equity built up, I was able to purchase some condos. Lets now access the pros and cons of renting out condos.

The Condo

Because of condo fees, taxes (property, school and water-sewer), mortgage payments and insurance, your costs are already high. Here is a hypothetical example of monthly expenses of a condo in a high-density area: condo fees around $400/month, insurance, $25, taxes, $200, loan $700, totaling $1325 a month. Rent may be just slightly higher than the total expenses, so, until your loan is paid off, all your rent money will go to carrying the place. Even once it's paid off, the net amount will not be as much as the income from renting two apartments in a house. I would guestimate that, once a condo is paid off, the net income, after expenses, is approximately half the rent.

The important point here is that repairs are much less for a condo than for a house. The owners of the building are responsible for anything that goes wrong with the structure or the roof. They use the money from the condo fees for repairs. Repairs for your unit consist of perhaps a plumber once every few years and a paint job from time to time.

When purchasing a condominium, be sure to find out how much is in the 'Reserve Fund'. A few years ago the government passed laws that every condo had to have a certain amount in reserve for high expenditures. Ascertain what improvements, renovations or repairs the condominium owners are planning in the near future.

The same financial formula exists as with a house if you have a line of credit.

The big risk, although a low probability, for owning a condominium is when the building needs a major re-haul. The condo owners share these costs. It could be several tens of thousands of dollars. Although this has never happened to me, I have heard of it happening to other people. It would be impossible to sell it with such a heavy lien on the property. So you pretty much have to come up with the money. Granted you should recuperate the costs when you sell as the value of the condo would have increased because of the improvements, but you would have to be able to come up with the money at the time. The same tax advantages apply as all costs are tax deductible including the interest on your loan.

Conclusion

Whatever you decide, the property should be up to code for health, safety and building standards so it behooves you to check these requirements out. The electrical, plumbing and heating have to be operational and safe. The building inspection will determine if you need to do any work in these areas. The bungalows I used as my accommodation and for rental, met the necessary safety measures. For example, the humidity levels were, for the most part, healthy, there was adequate ventilation, escape routes were accessible and clear and the general condition of the dwelling was decent. I didn't put in fire walls or other things that may be required for an apartment building.

Don't forget the laws about smoke detectors and be sure to have the required number for your rental units. You may procure an EPC, an Energy Performance Certificate, to show property is energy efficient. I never did this, but check if it is a requirement in your Municipality.

This comparison between owning a house or a condo gives you some idea of what you can expect in both situations. Hopefully, this information will help you decide which one is best for you.

CHAPTER FOUR

Risks vs Benefits of Owning Rental Property

Once you have decided what type of property is the one that most appeals to you and you are almost ready to bite the bullet, you still have to assess the risk-benefit ratio. It has been my experience that, even though there are risks, the benefits outweigh them. When launching on an adventure such as this that involves your money and credit, there are some things to consider that can minimize risk.

Get good tenants. A sound relationship with reliable tenants is where you want to be. Tenants can be a risk. Do your homework to research applicants and reduce your risk for problems.

Purchase a building with a sound infrastructure to avert possible future expenses. This basic principle is key to successful rental investment or property investment of any kind. If the infrastructure is sound, i.e. the foundation, the walls, the roof, the floors, the plumbing, the electrical, then there should be no big surprises and expenses would be for maintenance and voluntary improvements.

Maintain your investment. If you take care of the property as you go along, chances are you will avoid huge costs in the future.

I always took care of my properties just as I would the home I was living in. You want to have loyal tenants, ones who will respect your property. What helps to achieve this is keeping the place up and not letting it get run down. You don't want to be a slum landlord. When they feel you respect them and their residence, they tend to follow suit, hopefully.

Have enough money coming in. The financial risk of buying rental property is in part minimized by ensuring the rental income more than covers the principal and interest of the loan, taxes and insurance and repairs.

Have financial backup. When you first start out as a landlord, it is imperative that you have back up funds to protect your investment. If you have bad tenants who decide not to pay the rent, you need to have the funds there to cover the loan payments, or in the case of a line of credit, the monthly interest payments, for at least 3 to 4 months, as it may take you that long to evict them. There may be other unforeseen expenses and you must be prepared for them right from the outset.

The benefits of having rental property are long term ones. Ideally, the rent eventually pays for the property and for improvements over the years. After 15 or 20 years I estimate there will be a supplemental income after the loan is paid and a sizable profit on the original investment from the increased value of the property. The tax-deductible expenses along the way help reduce your total taxable income. These are big benefits one doesn't get from a GIC, a Mutual Fund or a bond.

Monies invested over the same period of time in a GIC, bonds or mutual funds, would grow, but they would not provide these tax advantages and you would be paying taxes on the interest. The invested amount would likely not grow as much as a property would, so, in the end, one would supposedly have more of an increase in equity in one's investment with property than one would with money in the bank.

When the property is sold, there will be capital gains to pay, but one will likely still be ahead of the game, barring the unforeseen. Nothing is guaranteed. We can't see into the future for whatever calamity might befall the economy, but taking the standard criteria into play, it is probable to turn out to be a benefit in the end.

Factors Affecting House Prices

House prices can fluctuate; they don't always go up, as we'd like to think. I believe, for the next while at least, boom times are over in real estate. You can gain, but you can lose, too. The most hoped for scenario is that house prices will stabilize and we will not see the insane increases of the past few decades.

Examining the factors affecting house prices will help you evaluate the risk involved. In the long spectrum of things, buying and renting out a house long term can be financially advantageous even if the equity doesn't go up significantly. You still have a house and it is being carried by the rent. I always argued to myself, it doesn't matter if the house is worth a dollar, if it's bringing in $1,000 a month, that's all I care about. What is important is to hang on to it and, if you have to sell, sell it in a stable market so at least you recoup your original investment. With any luck, you'll do that or better.

A basic stipulation of home pricing is the state of repair of the residence. **Curb appeal** will add value, as will a well-maintained property.

A demographic at play today is the **Baby Boomer generation**. In Canada they number around 10 million. When one reflects on the escalating prices of real estate over the last 40 some odd years, one can see there is a direct correlation between the Baby Boomers arriving at an age to settle down, have a family and buy a house, and the spike in house prices, which began in the early 1970's. Over the past few decades, they were buying and selling to each other. Like a tidal wave hitting the market place, the first batch of Boomers bought their beginner home, then later sold it to the next batch who were coming up behind them, allowing them to move up to a larger home, pushing up house prices with the increase in demand.

The time has come when the Boomers are downsizing from large to smaller homes, in particular, bungalows. Some will be going directly into a retirement home or into a condominium and others will just simply pass on. One would suspect that this would leave a glut of homes in the market, softening up house prices and likely boost the price of bungalows and condos. Immigration cannot replace this number of people moving out of the housing market. As this plays itself out, house prices may even decrease. The rush seems to be over as the Baby Boomers move through and out of the housing market.

Increases in mortgage interest rates or the **shortening of mortgage amortization periods** could increase the financial burden on a household's struggling budget and can subsequently slow down the housing market and depress prices.

Another factor to consider is the **unemployment rate**. If people are losing their jobs, they won't be able to keep their homes. This will drive prices down too and at the same time increase the demand for renting. Keep an eye on your area and see the unemployment rate as one barometer of the strength of the economy and how this affects house prices.

The **world economy** has a domino effect on our economy. If stock prices are falling and countries economies are failing, we will feel it too. Assess if the time is right to get into the housing market. But keep in mind, that, if you are looking at a long-term investment, these shorter-term indicators may not be so important.

CHAPTER FIVE

Finding the Tenant

Finding a good tenant, as previously pointed out, is another fundamental key in surviving proprietorship. You have to be discerning when screening prospective tenants. Having a feeling of trust and a sense that the person is sincere, solvent and reliable are very important.

Advertising

You can reach prospective tenants by using the free advertising sites on the Internet and local newspapers which offer free advertising. I found posting flyers around town, too, was a very successful way of finding tenants.

One doesn't have to spend a lot of money on advertising when these free services are available. You could even do a YouTube video of the rental unit and give the YouTube address plus your contact information in your ad or flyer.

Likewise, if you have a web site, you could take pictures of your property and post them on your site and put the web address in your ads. For a paying ad in a local newspaper, putting in your web address or YouTube video shortens the ad, gives all the information necessary and costs much less than describing everything in full.

In the ad, stick to explaining the premises and don't gear the ad to a particular group, such as 'ideal for retired couple'. This can be seen as discriminatory, so just explain the product. One can decide on the desirable tenant in the interview process.

You can always do it the old fashioned way and just stick a 'for rent' sign in the window.

The Applicants

When you advertise you have a place to rent, you are going to get all types responding to your ad. You may get people who just don't have the money to pay the rent, some may be into illegal activities such as drugs or dealing in 'hot' items, or, there may be some other factor that gets caught on your radar, such as dangerous or exotic pets. These are legitimate reasons not to rent to someone.

So how do you weed out the unwanted without looking discriminatory? There are a number of restrictions I would bring up to discourage undesirable renters from wanting my place. If they have pets, I'd say pets aren't allowed. If they were more than two, I'd say two is the maximum. Sometimes there just isn't room for more than two. I had a man come with his wife 100 kilometers from where he worked with their 6 kids to rent a 2-bedroom condo. I tried to explain there just wasn't room and it was against fire regulations. They eventually agreed. I wondered how they could even have considered it in the first place.

No children would be another restriction for me because of the nature of the accommodation; but you are not allowed to say that. I owned a condo in an adult community and I would have been shot at high noon in front of the post office if I had rented to this single mom with three kids. I explained this building was for retired people and there were no young families. She, in the end, decided it wouldn't be great for the kids. This became her decision not to take the apartment and not mine. I have on occasion reviewed the applicant's resume info and just outright told them they wouldn't be happy here, that it isn't the right place for them. If you are sharing your house, you can be more discerning as more restrictions are allowed in selecting a tenant.

One has to be so careful about not looking discriminating. Follow the law, wherever you live. It has to be the applicant's decision not to rent, so they need information that would make the unit undesirable for them, or you can say you've rented it to someone else. We are not allowed to discriminate, but I always believed I had the last say in who would be living in my property . . . . I could always think of something to make them decide the place wasn't for them, thus avoiding any accusations of being discriminating.

Screening the Applicant

Unfortunately, there are people who have had time to study the rental laws and take advantage of the loopholes. They know how to get free rent and even how to get paid by suing you. You don't want one of them as your tenant.

You have to be very aware of the landlord-tenant laws or you may find yourself an unsuspecting, uninformed landlord whom a piranhic tenant will eat alive. Because some landlords have been so bad in the past, laws have been passed to protect tenants, and rightly so. What is not so right is that the courts can favor the tenant. You don't want to be spending a lot of time in court.

How do you protect yourself from being a victim landlord? You have to rely on your intuition and better judgment, get a good person for a tenant in the first place and know the laws. Your priorities are that the tenant can pay the rent, that he is willing to follow the terms of the lease and that he will not destroy your place or use it for illegal or un-agreed upon activities.

Be sure to check him out thoroughly. Call past landlords, bosses and contact the character references. Verify his income by asking for pay stubs and clear him with the bank. (See 'Lease')

Applicants on Social Programs

For applicants on a social program, such as disability or welfare, I would arrange to have the rent deducted at source because they do not have a secure financial base. Since collecting the rent is your main concern, you have to protect your interest. It can be arranged that the government or agency will pay you before they issue their welfare cheque to the tenant. This protects you first. Paying the rent to the landlord before sending off the cheque to the recipient is done as a matter of course in some social welfare programs.

I always reserved the right to accept an applicant or not. The number one concern of mine is to have the rent paid. If I feel that is compromised and the applicant does not have the funds to pay the rent, I proceed to the next applicant. Besides which, lack of ability to pay the rent is a legitimate reason not to take someone as a tenant.

Pets and Children

Young working couples tend to want pets and possibly a family, so even though they may move in as two, they could become four or five very quickly. Some places are just not big enough for more than 2 people. Even a single man or woman may not be single very long, which is fine, except young people like to have pets and eventually will probably have children. What is the maximum capacity of your unit? If it is clear at the onset that the maximum is two, problems will be alleviated. If children do arrive on the scene, the tenants will know in advance that they have to find larger accommodation.

Even though everyone says they have the perfect dog and the cat that is kitty litter trained, this is simply not so. I would avoid people who have pets altogether. The only time you have any say about pets is before they move in.

If applicants have a pet and your place is not pet friendly, you don't have to accept them. But once they move in, it becomes illegal to evict them because they have a pet. If you do allow pets, make it clear they are the tenant's responsibility. You can always say 'no pets' in the lease. This includes exotic pets like boa constrictors. Yes, there are people who like tarantulas, rats even. Since tenants may not have pets when they are interviewed but get them after they move in, I have a special regulation in the lease that motivates them to take care of my property and to be responsible for their pets, which helps but doesn't guarantee anything. You can say in the lease that they pay more rent if they have a pet and remind them they are responsible to leave the place clean when they move out. The pet has to be removed if it is creating a disturbance, causing damage or causing allergic reactions.

I love animals and have given lots of leeway to my tenants, always with regrets. Cats are the worst. If they have a go at your carpets, you will likely have to replace them. I had one tenant in a basement apartment whose cat was alone all day and rebelled by marking his territory in every room. Another cat that belonged to a respectable retired policeman clawed the carpet up in the dining room all along the entrance to the kitchen. I've had fewer problems with dogs. Damage done by pets has to be paid for by the tenant and if they are destructive, there is a procedure in place to evict them.

So be cautious about pets and be clear about the number of allowable occupants when interviewing.

The Ideal Tenant

I've been told that the best, most reliable tenants are the retired who live alone. They pay their bills and want security. They don't cause any trouble and are long term. I got this secret from a rich real estate mogul in Ottawa. First rule, rent to the retired and, second rule, don't sell. With the aging population, there are lots of eligible tenants out there. I feel many people can be ideal tenants. The most ideal tenant is one who will take care of the place and pay the rent.

CHAPTER SIX

The Lease

When I began as a landlord, I had very little information on renting, legal or otherwise. I found out more about the laws as I gained experience, but to start, I was never very concerned about them, either because I was too naive or because I didn't anticipate that I'd have many problems and, luckily for me, it turned out to be pretty much the way things went. There were exceptions, though, unfortunately.

I had the attitude that I'd take care of my tenants and my property and they would be good tenants and pay the rent. But the road to hell can be paved with high expectations, so I am not recommending anyone follow this example, but rather be prepared by being familiar with the law, both with the landlord and tenant laws and the local bylaws. You don't want to be outsmarted by one of those tenants who knows the law better than you and milks it for all its worth at your expense. With a good lease, a good tenant and knowledge of the laws, one hopes to avoid any unwanted court cases.

My lease is the result of the information and the experience that I have gained over the years. I prepared it and brought it to a lawyer to ensure it was legally acceptable. A lot of thought and research went into it.

As time went on, I adjusted it for specific tenants, but it served as my core lease. I tried to cover as many areas as I could to avert future misunderstandings. The lease is an agreement between the landlord and the tenant. I felt it should mutually serve all parties. Here is where I could clarify my expectations of the tenant, behaviors he was to abide by, and itemize what I was willing to do for him. Although we sign such an agreement, it does not go beyond the letter of the law. For me, I always hoped that the lease served all parties sufficiently and there would never be a reason to challenge it. It works for me. Basically, my job is to ensure the property is safe. Their job is to take care of it and pay the rent.

The landlord and tenant can come to an oral agreement, which is binding, but due to weak memories and personal perspectives, it is always better to have a written lease with very clear terms.

Terms of the Lease:

Address: [address of rental property, street, town, Province and postal code]
Owner:
Contact number:
Type of dwelling: [Bungalow] [Condominium]
Maximum number of people:
Date of Occupancy:
Term of the Lease:

The first thing I request from the prospective tenant is a list of information. They must provide a **police report**. This eliminates unsavory candidates because those who have a shady record usually don't go any further. If an applicant did have a police record, this did not always deter me from renting to them, as the contraventions may have been minor, such as traffic violations. I sometimes would give a person a chance if they had a former record of drug abuse but had a convincing argument that they are reformed. This, of course is risky but one has to trust one's own judgment. By having a police report, at least I know a little bit more about the person in order to make a decision.

I need a photocopy of both sides of their **driver's license**. This is necessary to verify their ID and to have on hand in the eventuality of a police incident or an issue with the law.

I request **three reference letters** with phone numbers: a job reference letter from the current employer, a letter from the second last landlord and a character reference from someone other than a relative. I ask for a reference from the second last landlord because he doesn't have a vested interest in recommending them. He will have knowledge of their behavior as a tenant, if they pay the rent on time and if they are respectful of the rules.

It is not advisable to only get a reference from the last landlord because maybe he can't wait to get rid of them and will say anything to encourage you to take on his problem tenants. Make sure that the character reference is someone who has known the person for at least 5 years, not a new best friend of 3 weeks who is 15 years old. Have the tenant sign that he is authorizing you to contact these references so you can validate yourself as a landlord when you contact them.

Although I am entitled to do a complete **credit check**, I usually just ask for a letter from their bank stating that they are clients in good standing. If you wanted to do a complete credit check, you could pay *Equifax* or *Trans Union*, credit-reporting agencies, to do one for you. They will provide you with information about bills paid on time or late or not paid at all.

I request they get a ***Tenant Insurance Package***. This costs less than $200.00 and offers protection of their personal belongings in an adverse event such as fire or flooding. Their things are their responsibility. My responsibility is to take care of the building and provide them with a safe dwelling.

Further information requested includes: present address, length of time there, reason for leaving, landlord's name and phone number, previous landlords information, job information, boss's phone number, salary and other sources of income, length of time at the job, bank information and a bank statement showing monthly deposits of income. I provide a form for them to fill in for this information

The lease must be returned to me with all the requested information plus a cheque for first and last month's rent and **11 post dated cheques** for the year. If they leave at the end of the lease, I return the 12th cheque to them as they have already paid for the last month. I give them a receipt for the cheques and I photocopy them for my files.

By law one can't demand post-dated cheques, but all my tenants have done so and haven't had a problem with the request. I explain in the lease that the bank handles the cheques and any NSF cheques will have a detrimental impact on their credit rating. By getting post-dated cheques for the year, I do not have to chase the rent money. I leave them with **the bank** and they deposit them regularly at the beginning of each month.

You could decide on a late payment fee. I make it clear that if the rent is not paid on time, then that month will be considered the last month of tenancy and they would be required to leave by the end of the month. In the event of **default of rent** and it's settled in court, the tenant is responsible to pay the rent in default, legal fees and other costs incurred by the landlord in collecting such rent. There are forms (from the Landlord and Tenant Board) to fill out for notification of eviction, but more on that later.

The **rent increase** will not be more than the amount set by the Ontario Government, usually not more that 2.5%.

Further stipulations in the lease include a request that they must **keep the property in the same good condition** that it was in when they arrived. They must not leave anything blocking entrances or lying around outside like beer bottles, trash or large garbage-like items. Here I cite Bylaws to back up these requests and point out that any costs incurred for clean up will be passed on to them.

Explain local **garbage collection** practices.

It is their responsibility to keep the unit **reasonably clean** and to take reasonable care of the place. Extermination of bed bugs etc. will be at the renter's expense since they weren't there when they moved in.

They must respect the right of **quiet and privacy of the neighbors.** I cite the Bylaws and the tenants' financial responsibility if they violate them.

If it is a condo rental, they must review and follow the rules and regulations, of which I leave them a copy.

Mention there are to be no unusually large items such as a waterbed or large appliances brought into the rental unit.

Appliances provided in the unit are their responsibility. For example, there may be a dishwasher, fridge, washer, dryer, but it is up to the tenant to maintain them.

I clarify **what they have to pay for**, such as hydro, gas, water and what is included in the rent, such as parking and laundry.

I explain what area of the house is **shared**, normally the laundry area.

The duration of the **lease is 12 months**, but the **first 3 months is a trial period**. Upon satisfactory inspection of the property and tenancy, the lease will be validated for the remaining 9 months. This trial period gives them a chance to decide if they like it or not and they are free to move if the accommodation doesn't suit them. It also gives me a chance to fine-tune their tenancy.

I've never had to tell a tenant that it wasn't working out and that they had to leave, but the above clause would give me that leeway. I've always used it as an opportunity to discuss how the apartment is working for them and to review if they are adhering to the terms of the lease.

If a tenant wants to break the lease, I require **two months notice**. The law says that a tenant can move out only after the term of the lease is over, but to me, it doesn't make good sense. I don't want tenants in my property who don't want to be there, so they are able to leave with two months written notice. Therefore, there are no subletting or assignment clauses in the lease.

For the size of my apartments, mostly two-bedroom, I limit the occupancy to **two persons**. If another person moves in, then I state in the lease that the rent goes up $50.00 to $100 a month.

There are to be **no changes to the property,** such as painting, installing a satellite dish, cutting branches or damaging trees, hedges or bushes without the landlord's written consent.

The landlord must authorize, in writing, any use of the property other than for residential or, as stated in the lease.

I always felt one should be rewarded for a job well done and my tenants were no exception. I state that if they follow the terms of the lease and they are good tenants, they receive a **bonus** of between $300 and $600 each year after 12 months of tenancy. Any damage done to the property must be rectified to secure the bonus. I include this bonus because I feel that deserving tenants should have a return on their money.

I used their money to pay my loan and improve the property, so I believe they should get some encouragement for being good tenants. This bonus motivates them to take care of the property and follow the terms of the lease. I believe it is the core of the success I have had in renting. It helps develop loyalty and it is much cheaper than going to court to settle a dispute. There will be an inspection when they leave and to get the bonus, the unit must be left as clean as when they moved in.

In the case of a house, I would state that they are responsible for **lawn care and snow removal.**

I make it clear that this is a **non-smoking residence and there are to be no pets**. If you have a 'no pet' policy and an applicant has a pet, that would be grounds to not take them as a tenant. If they move in and then get pets, you can only complain to *'the Board'* if the pet causes damage as per the *'Residential Tenancies Act'*. You could make it clear that if they do have pets, they pay more rent.

I clarify that I will give **24 hours notice** when I want to see the unit between the hours 8 a.m. to 8 p.m. I confirm that I am available 24 hours a day at the given contact number.

Finally, I say that the lease agreement can be amended at any time at the discretion of the landlord.

I end the lease with "I fully understand the conditions of this rental agreement and I acknowledge that failure to adhere to these conditions will be grounds for eviction by the owner. **I accept** this rental agreement with this understanding."

When all the requested information has been submitted to me, we **review the terms of the lease together before signing**. There would be two copies, one for each party involved.

The tenant and the landlord mutually agree to the terms in the lease by signing the rental agreement. Keep in mind that if the lease has a stipulation inconsistent with the *'Residential Tenancies Act'* (referred to as 'the Act'), or with the *'Landlord and Tenant Board'* (referred to as *'the Board'*), the courts will not enforce it in the event of a dispute.

It's always a good idea to go into the premises with the tenant before they move in and make a written **list of the condition of the unit**. Record in writing and if possible, with photos, all marks and dents, and the condition of the windows, walls and appliances.

It's a good idea to have a checklist of the do's and don'ts' for the unit. Review simple things like how the plumbing and electrical systems work, including changing light bulbs and cleaning or replacing the furnace filter.

It is required to tell the prospective tenant before they move in, about the *'Landlord and Tenant Board'* and about the rights and responsibilities of both the tenant and of the landlord. *'The Board'* has a brochure available for this purpose, **"Information for New Tenants"**, which you must provide. Make it clear that if they are evicted for violating any part of the lease, that they will pay damages, back rent and court fees.

You can ask for a security deposit, which you will put aside. You return this, with interest, at the end of the tenancy. Money can only be deducted from the deposit for damages done to the property.

The lease is **renewed** every year. If the lease is not renewed in writing, it becomes a month-to-month lease and the same terms of the rental agreement apply.

The tenant can terminate the lease at the end of the rental period giving 60 days written notice, or before, if mutually agreed upon with the landlord. Form **N11,** *'Agreement to Terminate a Tenancy'*, from *the 'Board'*, can be filled out or the landlord and tenant can make an oral agreement concerning lease termination; however, it's always better to get such agreements in writing.

N.B. If the tenant has to move out early, he can either sublet the unit, in which case the landlord reserves the right to agree on the new tenant, or, the tenant can assign the lease to another person and that person takes over the lease until it is ended. This is called 'an assignment'. These choices exist in the law, but as I explained, I don't deal with sublets or assignments because the tenants are permitted to leave when they give due notice.

Rent Increase

When I have a good tenant, I may not increase the rent for the first two or three years. When there is a rent increase, it can only be on the date of renewal of the lease and it must be in accordance with the Government limit for that year. The rent cannot be increased in the first year or first 12 months of the rental period.

The landlord should give the tenant 90 days notice of a rent increase. Form **N1**, (page 106) from *the 'Board'*, is used for rent increase notification, but a properly formed letter would also serve the purpose. This allows the tenant to decide if they want to stay or not and gives them time to submit a letter of intent to leave within the 60 day guideline.

Rent increases can be around 2.5% a year depending on the cost of living index or the *'Consumer Price Index'*, set by the Ontario Government. Each year by August 31st, the Government announces the guideline for rent increases for January 1st of the next year. The *'Landlord and Tenant Board'* must approve any rent increase over the set amount announced for that year by the Government. Rent cannot be increased over 3% of the rent received the previous year.

Small Repairs and Insurance Claims

It is always a bonus to have a tenant who is handy to do small repairs. Most of the time, this will not be the case, so it would be advisable to have a reliable handyman on call if the landlord cannot do the jobs himself. It pays off in the long run for you to keep up with the small repairs because it is your property and, besides, the law says you have to. Proper maintenance benefits you because it maintains the property value, provides tax deductions on materials and labor and keeps your tenants happy. I would recommend that you attend to these small repairs as quickly as possible.

When you insure your property, be sure to inform the insurance company that your property is a rental property. They will cover you accordingly and give you extra liability coverage for personal injury. The rates are not all that much more, so it is not something you should avoid. Be sure you are fulfilling all their requirements because you want coverage of your investment in case of a disaster. They could refuse to pay if you haven't followed their guidelines. In the event of major damage, such as a sump pump backing up, or flooding, or even fire, you have your insurance covering your property and, as mentioned previously, your tenant should have his 'Tenant Insurance Package' to cover damage to his personal belongings.

CHAPTER SEVEN

The Landlord and Tenant Board

'*The Landlord and Tenant Board*', was created by the '*Residential Tenancies Act*' *to* give residential landlords and tenants rights and responsibilities and to set out a process as to how these can be enforced. '*The Board*' is there to resolve landlord-tenant disputes either through a process of mediation, which allows discussion between the parties with the help of a mediator, or by adjudication, that would be by a judgment issued by '*the Board*'. '*The Board*' also provides forms to be filled out in the case of a conflict such as non-payment of rent or eviction and provides guidelines for rent increases.

Of course if you have a dispute with a tenant as a landlord, it could mean looking at ending the tenancy early. This process is like touching a hot stove; you likely will not wish to experience it too often. There is a certain aversion one has to dealing with such rental issues, as it is so unpleasant to have to evict a tenant. But, you have to know the process and know what to do in the event that you have to terminate the lease.

Early Termination of Lease

A landlord may terminate the lease early for:

* non-payment of rent
* late payment of rent
* for tenants damaging the property
* having too many persons in the unit
* disturbing the landlord or other tenants, being a nuisance
* for interfering with the landlords or other tenants 'reasonable enjoyment'
* for breaking terms in the lease
* in the event they are conducting illegal activity in the unit.

The 'no fault' reasons for eviction include:

* the necessity of major repairs
* the landlord or his family is moving into the unit
* a purchaser of the landlord's property requires the place for his family.

(These last two restrictions apply only to properties of three units or less or condominiums.)

The road to evict a tenant is costly, stressful, rocky and filled with potential delays. You have to fill forms properly, provide the right information and follow the procedures to the letter. It is reassuring to know that you are not legally bound to be stuck with an undesirable tenant and that the law does protect landlords from tenants who don't pay the rent, who live an illegal lifestyle or who are disruptive or destructive. They have to get out. Of course, you can lose several months rent in the process, but you will get rid of them. They would be required to pay rent due and court costs, but collecting the money is another story.

'The Board' has forms for the landlord to fill out and time lines to follow. If, for example, your tenant is not paying the rent, you have to start proceedings. First of all, I would have made it clear in the lease that if the rent were not paid by the first of the month, then I am to assume it is their last month. Proceedings have to be started immediately. Don't wait on this as it just drags things out at the other end as your tenant sits there and has free rent for yet another month. You could discuss with him the fact that you will report him as a bad tenant risk to the Credit Bureau. This may motivate him to pay up. Eviction is the last avenue. It is always better to try and resolve issues calmly and reasonably before starting the eviction process.

Eviction Procedure: Steps to follow to evict a tenant for one of the above listed reasons

Summary:

1. Serve Notice to tenant
2. Initiate eviction process
3. Wait for court date
4. Notify tenant of hearing date
5. Attend hearing
6. Get eviction order
7. If tenant refuses to leave: Enforce eviction: Court Enforcement Office and the Sheriff

You will have to get the necessary forms for your Province or State. These are the procedures for Ontario.

1. Fill out **Form N4** (page 82) correctly, '*Notice to End a Tenancy Early for Non-Payment of Rent*': this explains the reason for eviction. It gives 14 days notice starting the following day you serve the notice. In this time, the tenant has the opportunity to rectify the problem. The form requires you name each person in the unit. State the amount of money owing and include the address. **The landlord can serve the N4 the day after the rent was due.** The N4 form includes guidelines to properly fill out the form. This form gives the tenant 14 days to pay the rent and informs him that if the rent is not paid in this time frame, then he will be served with eviction papers.

2. Fill out **Form L1** (page 85), an '*Application to Evict the Tenant for Non-payment of Rent and to Collect Rent the Tenant Owes*', and pay $170.00. **This can be filed the day after the N4 runs out** called the termination date. The tenant will be required to reimburse the landlord's costs of the eviction process as well as pay the rent arrears. Be aware that even though the courts may rule that the tenant is to pay these expenses, collection is another matter and more often than not, the money is not secured.

[The landlord can solely request the rent be paid and not want to evict the tenant. In this case the form to fill out would be *'Application to Collect Rent the Tenant Owes'*, **Form L9** (page 96).]

3. When *'the Board'* processes Form **L1** (page 85) for eviction, a **hearing** will be scheduled. **The tenant must receive notification in writing or copies of the hearing date 10 days or more before the hearing.**

At the hearing, *'the Board'* provides mediation beforehand to help the landlord and tenant come to a satisfactory agreement. This is voluntary. After the hearing, the eviction notice can be nullified if the tenant reimburses the landlord the court fees plus pays the rent owing. If the tenant is ordered to pay the rent and court fees and refuses, you have to take him to Small Claims Court to collect. It's one thing to get the order and another to collect.

4. **A resolution can be arrived at through an 'adjudication'**, which is a judgment issued at the hearing based on evidence presented by the landlord and the tenant. *'The Board'* makes a decision that is called 'an order'. It is the final written decision of *'the Board'* that both the landlord and tenant must adhere to.

5. **If the tenant is non-compliant, the eviction order can be filed with the Sheriff's Office.** The landlord files the eviction order with the Court Enforcement Office. The Sheriff can lock the tenant out and force him to respect the eviction notification. When the tenant refuses to move out, only the sheriff can evict them with an order form *'the Board'*.

Tenants can be evicted in the winter months for violating the lease of the law. The process is the same at any time of the year.

Forms can be downloaded from the net or picked up at Service Ontario Offices (in Ontario). Some forms have been included at the end of this book. Keep copies of all forms and register dates that they have been completed. You may need them in court.

CHAPTER EIGHT

Responsibilities of the Landlord

Responsibilities of The Landlord

You must be very clear on these responsibilities. If you don't know the law, and your tenant does, he may not be nice about it and, if that turns out to be the case, you will pay dearly. For clarity, I'm going to list some key things that you must do for your tenant. If you follow these guidelines based in law, (others may exist) you will be protecting yourself from the renting to Hyde, (the bad one). If you don't know the law, and just take your chances, you could find yourself in the category of a 'victim' landlord. So here are some major requirements:

- You must provide your tenant with hot and cold running water
- You must provide adequate heat, electrical and plumbing
- There must be adequate heat ventilation
- Windows and doors must be adequate for weather conditions in all seasons
- Ceilings, walls and lights must be up to standard
- You must abide by safety codes for fire and health
- You must maintain the property, shared areas like hallways, common rooms, entrances
- You are responsible for lawn care and snow removal unless agreed otherwise in the lease
- You must provide a copy of the lease and receipts of rent paid
- At no time are you able to change the locks
- You are not to enter unit illegally
- You are not to harass your tenant
- You cannot cut off essential services like heat, electricity, water

If you violate any terms of the lease of or the laws that protect tenants, you could be faced with large penalties, one of which is a fine of $10,000 to the *Landlord and Tenant Board*. You will be responsible to replace any and all property of your tenant that has been damaged due to your negligence. If your tenant has to move out due to your actions, then you will be responsible to pay expenses incurred by this move, such as, moving, storage, any increase in rent at the new place for one year and any other 'reasonable' expenses.

Commercial rentals

There are fewer laws in place to protect tenants in commercial rentals. Eviction times are shorter and regulations are more brutal for the tenant. For example, if a commercial tenant is evicted, he may be responsible to pay the rent for the remaining time of the lease even though he has moved out of the rental property. You need much more money to get into commercial real estate, but, apparently, the landlord has more control over the tenant and the terms of the lease.

The purpose of this book is to impart information for residential property rentals. If you would like to know more about being a commercial landlord, here is a site that may give you some tips: http://www.caltenantlaw.com/ Bus-Law.htm#Golden (You may have to copy and paste it)

CHAPTER NINE

Keeping Records

It is advisable to have a good tax accountant to do your taxes, one who is well versed in rental real estate tax laws.

I keep track of my business and expenses by meticulously keeping receipts and entering them in a ledger. At tax time I give the ledger and the receipts to the accountant. It is way too complicated for me, and these tax accountants are up to date on the latest tax laws. I have a lot of confidence to let them do the work for me.

Aside from the tax part of my business, I keep a binder on each property, with a section for each concern, such as copies of the rent cheques, copy of the lease and correspondence, written or oral, with the tenant, hydro, phone, taxes, bank statements, loan information, a chronology of dates and times of events concerning the property, complaints, repairs, warranties and owners manuals. Keep all forms and statements and file them carefully.

Organizing the information on my properties in the binders allows me to get my hands on information very quickly.

It's a good idea to have a name of a lawyer who specializes in landlord-tenant issues. Be clear, preferably in writing, as to the fees he charges and what you can expect to pay to get advice from him.

Tax Deductions, A Review

- Insurance
- Maintenance and repairs
- Property taxes
- Accountants fees
- Advertising
- Services: gardening, cleaning
- Utilities
- Interest on loan
- Travel expenses if property out of town
- Legal fees
- Phone expenses
- Business expenses (equipment, accessories)
- Fees: legal, condo, real estate

CHAPTER TEN

Expect the Best, But Be Prepared for the Worst:
The Jekyll and Hyde of Owning Rental Property

The names have been changed to protect the guilty.

Remember we talked about the dream and the nightmare? I have to admit, I have been very fortunate with my tenants, even though I have had a few 'winners'. I'd like to share with you the realities of being a landlord by recounting experiences I've had as well as some disconcerting stories from my sister, Susan.

Let's keep in mind that the intelligence of the group of tenants renting your property is equivalent to that of the least intelligent tenant. This level would be higher than the landlord who is standing outside the adjudicator's office at the hearing of '*the Board*', required to pay $10,000 to '*the Board*' for violating an unbeknownst-to-him law that protects tenants, in addition to paying three months rent to the tenants, their moving expenses, storage fees and future increases in their rent. This can happen if the landlord has violated a ruling or a clause in the lease. He becomes responsible to cover expenses the tenant incurs due to his actions.

The other side of the coin of victim landlords, is that scum landlords have forced into existence entities such as *"The Landlord and Tenant Board"* to protect people who have to rent from them. It is a good thing. Vulnerable people can't be out there trying to have a life in an unfit rental place at the mercy of some unreasonable scoundrel landlord. What is not a good thing is when the law favors renters unreasonably at the expense of the owner. It's the old adage of the pendulum swinging. The poor protection tenants previously had from bad landlords has caused the pendulum to swing to the extreme in the other direction of sometimes protecting the tenants at the expense of the landlord. Although this may not necessarily cause financial ruin for the landlord, any reduction in income could really hurt his pocket book and temporarily maim him.

The Tenants

My first few tenants were ideal. One couple shared my bungalow with me, and other tenants rented separate bungalow apartments or condos. I had a retired gentleman for 8 years renting a condo and all he requested was a plumber once or twice and the installation of a ceiling fan to alleviate the heat of the summers. I paid the taxes, insurance and condo fees and the bank put the post dated rent cheques into my account. This is the dream, the 'Jekyll' of renting. Tenants with whom I shared my residence were, in my experience, also dream tenants. It got a little sticky with a couple of my independent bungalow apartment renters.

Bob: drugs, pets, boarders

One fellow, let's call him Bob, was single, and ex-drug user as per his police report, and a turned-out-to-be, present drug user as well. He had a few issues with traffic violations, but was full of promises of reform and wanting a fresh start in his life and I wanted to give him a chance. He stayed for about 5 years in the lower level apartment. Even though he insisted he was a neat freak, the place gradually deteriorated. He had borders unauthorized by me, used extension cords and power bars to power numerous appliances and electrical gadgets, got a cat that was not kitty litter trained, continued his drug habit and moved furniture in that was larger than life. During periods when he was unemployed, I lowered the rent to help him out and hired him for odd jobs. He was polite with me and paid his rent, but he was bad tempered with other tenants and with the neighbors.

One visit found him out of sorts. He was moaning that the place wasn't fit to live in because of the high humidity levels. Well, he was right. The upstairs tenant had turned off the furnace fan, causing humidity to build up on the lower level. Mold had started to amass on the floorboards. I freaked. I wrote him a note stating I was concerned about his health and agreed the place should not be lived in and he should move out so I could investigate where the source of the problem was. I needed to take the walls down and see if there was a crack in the foundation. This sent him into a frenzy of anger against me. It was at this point he cancelled payment of the rent cheques and stayed there for two months. I call it squatting, but one is not to use this term anymore.

I served him with the proper papers for eviction for non-payment of rent and followed the due process and he eventually did leave. He took with him all the window coverings and the built in microwave and left garbage stuffed everywhere including gas-soaked and greasy things.

I did not follow through the legal process to collect the rent and damages because I believed he was a fly-by-night character and would not pay, even though he would be ordered to do so by '*the Board*' or by the Small Claims Court. It was just too much negative energy for me to put out for the probability of not being compensated. It was better I moved on, clean the place up and get a new tenant. This was my first "they'll wreck your place and not pay the rent" experience. But it worked for 5 years and that rent money helped me improve the property and pay the loan, so I was happy to forget his debt to me. I was just relieved he didn't burn the place down. You see, it could always be worse.

Garth, the retired cop

Another fun tenant I had was a retired policeman. This man, let's call him Garth, prided himself in his integrity and proudly handed me a stack of glowing reports on his exemplary character and accomplishments. Certainly a good bet for a tenant, you would think, being so integrous and liquid. He rented out the upper level of one of my bungalows and he had a partner. He had in mind to buy the place eventually so he was motivated to improve it. He forgot that he was only a tenant and that I was the owner for the time being. Also, his idea of improvement did not always agree with mine.

The first issue was the color of the inside of the house. I lived with a beautiful shade of gold. He asked that he paint it a pretty yellow. I didn't think the place needed painting, but if he were going to be owning it eventually, I conceded. The yellow he picked was more a canary yellow. Just glad I didn't have to live with it.

The privacy fence along the full side of the lot fell short about 15 feet of the back fence. Garth had a little puppy that was terrified of the two German Shepherds next door and wouldn't go outside. So Garth asked if he could complete the fence. I said sure he could and I would pay for the materials. He wasn't exactly a carpenter, but the job was done.

Next thing I knew, he had painted the front windows and front door. Good thing it was white and not some other color. He did this without asking permission, but it looked nice so I accepted it.

I noticed the giant ferns that lined the back of the house were removed and replaced with a vegetable garden. This was a totally shaded area where nothing but a shade plant would grow. I was surprised at the unintelligence of this decision and irritated that he did not ask for permission to remove my beautiful ferns.

That annoyance was small compared to the reaction I had when he removed 5 pines from the side of the house because they offered too much shade for the basement apartment. Frankly, I liked them for the privacy they gave and I felt enough light came through and I didn't find they darkened the apartment at all. In any event, the trees were gone, even though it stated in the lease that no trees were to be injured or cut. He had already violated this term of the lease by nailing nails into the cedar trees around the deck, for hanging garden ornaments.

And, oh yes, let's not forget the deck. One day I arrived to find it painted white. I pointed out that this was a big mistake on his part and that he should never have done that. He assured me he would remove the paint and put the cedar stain back, if and when he were to leave; which, when he didn't buy the house and did leave, he didn't do. It may have helped had I put the agreement in writing, but by not doing so, it made it easier for him to just walk away.

When I was looking for a tenant for the lower level apartment, Garth had a keen interest to meet the prospective tenant and interview them to be sure he would want them in the same house as he was living upstairs. I thought this was a reasonable request and he was certainly qualified to screen them. So he did a few interviews, but none panned out while he was there.

He complained about the white snowball bushes in the front of the house, that there were too many of them. I suggested I'd come over and take out two at least and use them elsewhere. When I arrived, I got shooed off the property as if I were an invader and told to respect his privacy, only to find after he moved out that he took them with him.

At one point I wanted to clean the apartment downstairs to prepare it for renting. Garth's partner, a Molly Maid employee, offered to clean it and I offered to give her $50.00 even though she didn't ask for payment. When they left the property, I let them store their corvette in the garage for $50 a month, only to find out they had taken advantage of the situation and had left other things besides the car, like a trailer full of their belongings and a garden tractor. The new tenants who moved in had to deal with these things until he finally came and removed them.

Before Garth and his partner moved out and after they decided not to buy the house, they presented me with a $10,000 bill for the work they had done and interviews they had conducted, which they interpreted as managerial fees. I was under no obligation to pay them because I had not asked them to do any work, but I dropped off a cheque for another $100 for the cleaning she had done.

They left after stopping payment on the last months rent and owing me $300 from previous rent. Again I did not pursue them in court. They had left me with damages over $5,000, including the rug the cat clawed, and the cost of removing their garbage in the garage. For that amount, it just wasn't worth the time and energy needed to take them to court, again and again and again. Garth left feeling justified not to compensate me because I was such a vile character and an abusive landlord. You see? Perspective is everything.

I learned to keep the tenancy separate from repairs and not to allow tenants to do work that is not required. Work to be done has to be in writing and it has to be clear who is to do it and who is paying for it. Never deduct payment for work from the rent. Keep it separate. They pay the rent. You pay them for work and get a receipt. I should never have allowed Garth to do the work. He had a false sense of proprietorship, which should have been squelched from the beginning.

My Sister, Susan's, Landlord Experiences

Wasn't it Murphy's Law that said anything that can go wrong, will? Well, the perfect example of this is the landlord adventures of my sister, Susan. Her experiences as a landlady would give anyone a bad case of hives. She is living proof that when one has a bad time renting out properties, one develops an extreme aversion to tenants, sells off their properties, puts their money in the bank and gets some sleep at night. It just took her a little longer than most to get the picture. Hence, she reminds me of Irma Brombeck who said her second most favorite thing was ironing, but her first most favorite thing was hitting her head over and over against the frame of the upper bunk bed until she fainted.

Phase One

You see, Susan, in her previous life as a hippie, was against capitalism, but for the oppressed, that included tenants of which she, herself, was one. She eventually rented a farm in the country for about 10 years where she ran a small equestrian riding business. Being concerned that when her lease was up she may be obliged to move, she thought she better find another place as a back up to run her business. She realized that she and her husband had enough put aside at this point for a down payment for a property of their own. So, off they went and bought a duplex on a lovely 100-acre property on the edge of a small town. However, in the end, they didn't need to move from the farm as the lease was renewed, leaving the duplex empty, just asking to be rented.

Looking back, Susan wishes she had listened to a couple of occurrences that she now sees as bad omens: running over the dog on one of the visits to the duplex, and her 'supportive' husband congratulating her on becoming 'A Scum Sucking Landlord.'

The first three years were the great years, the Dr. Jekyll of renting. God was rewarding Susan for all the years she herself had been the perfect tenant. When the tenants on both sides of the duplex moved out at the same time, the 'landlordom' of Hyde was waiting, unsuspectingly, just around the corner. When there was no money coming in to cover the mortgage, the family that arrived wanting to rent both sides of the duplex looked pretty good. In a panic, Susan signed them up. Win! Win! This virgin landlady was just about to get fudleduddled.

After a couple of months with no rent money coming in, Susan and her husband decided to take a run out and see what was up. The extension cord running out a window on one side into a window on the other side left them speechless and motionless in the car. Once they collected their bearings, they approached the tenants. Apparently hydro had been cut off on one side, so naturally they would run an extension cord from the side that had hydro to the side that didn't.

A screaming match ensued between Susan and the renters that resolved nothing. The dispute ended with Susan's husband saying he was having nothing more to do with the place.

Susan took the matter in her own hands and called Hydro. They didn't want to call on the tenants until Susan could produce their marriage certificate. As if she would just walk up and ask, "Can I please have your marriage certificate?" and they would say, "Well, of course, here you go. Now you can cut off our hydro!" Hydro did eventually pay a visit and all seemed okay because the tenants removed the extension cord when they were alerted Hydro was coming.

So now it was on to court. Susan was home schooling her two children, 2 and 4 and thought it would be beneficial to them, and part of their education, to see what it was like to go to court. So, there they sat with her, time and time again, on those hard benches. Improperly filled forms, no shows, dribbles of rent paid, all prolonged the court proceedings. Back and forth, back and forth she went, on the bus, with the kids. Finally, Susan got her eviction papers and the tenants had to leave.

That was her inauguration into the rental world as a landlord. It was only going to get better.

Phase Two

Next, a nice young couple rented one half of the duplex and a family on welfare rented the other half. Susan believed that social services would provide enough for rent and essentials. She was soon to discover that this was not the case. Upon visiting the unit of the welfare family, she was horrified to discover they were heating the place with the oven and the kids were wearing overcoats. She, in her mind, would become a verifiable 'Scum Sucking Landlord' if she insisted on taking rent money when they could not even afford heat. It was morally unconscionable.

And the nice couple on the other side had it all figured out. They stopped paying the rent promptly whenever they could find something on the 'you don't have to pay your rent IF" list. Such as mice. It was evident that both sides had to leave and they eventually did. Upon their vacating the premises, Susan had the mind-blocking job of cleaning up the mess of dried diapers, rat feces, house dirt and grease.

Phase Three

The next tenants were two couples, one on each side of the duplex. They looked as though they'd be perfect. It seemed 'landlordom' was going to regain its anticipated, 'Jekyll', status of decency. Until the fateful phone call came.

Something was wrong with the oil tank, as the basement was full of oil. This disaster predated the legislation that required concrete beds under oil tanks. The culprit was a corrosive puncture hole that dripped oil into the wall of the house, into the basement and out to the septic bed. Is this not a nightmare for any property owner? Well, this was not a bad dream. This was for real.

The oil company came and dispersed pellets to absorb the oil but that effort didn't have any effect. The insurance would only cover whatever was within the walls of the house, anything outside of that was not covered. The smell was pungent and pervasive.

At this point, to make matters worse, Susan's husband left her with the two kids for his secretary and gave her the place as a settlement. Her Mother had given her the second mortgage and, with the looming possibility of losing her money, was pressuring Susan to pay up.

The cleanup started with removal of the contaminated dirt away from the exterior wall. This caused the wall to crack once the support of the dirt was removed. The house itself was cleaned but the smell lingered. The 250 gallons of oil that had gone down the wall, across the floor and out to the septic bed, had to be dug up, at the cost of $50,000. Susan was still home schooling her children and now single. The Ministry of the Environment (MOE) said they would analyze and possibly approve the cleanup plan Susan submitted and the cost could be half of that estimate.

Because of bureaucratic incompetence, the insurance company (after another kind year of Jekyll) cut off her insurance because she was a bad homeowner who did not clean up this terrible oil spill. She argued, HEY! She had responsibly put the case in the hands of the MOE who never did get around to approving the cleanup plan she had submitted. After investigation, it turned out the MOE had lost the paperwork. In the meantime a nice family had moved in with the intention to rent to buy. After a year, they bought it for $50,000 less than Susan had paid for it and they took over the job of rectifying the oil problem.

Susan didn't care. With a sigh of relief she kissed 'landlordom' away. That was the end of that world of headaches. Or so she thought.

Susan shows:

<u>**THE CHARLIE BROWN SYNDROME**</u>

(Lucy: "Come on Charlie Brown, kick the football, I won't pull it away!" Charlie Brown runs to kick the ball, and you guessed it, Lucy yanks it away and Charlie falls on his back, yet again.)

Phase Four

A few years passed, savings accumulated from Susan's small, but thriving, business, and memory failed of the Hyde-ness of property ownership like the fading recollection of the pain of childbirth. Susan fell victim, once more, to the seduction of home ownership. The farm was on a beautiful concession, consisting of a barn and a house on 40 acres. Yes, Susan dreamed, she could retire in it and, until then, rent it out.

The day the house was signed over, the basement flooded for, apparently, the first time. If there were any way to rewind this day as in a bad video, Susan would have done it. But it was, for all intents and purposes, too late.

The first tenant dealt with the occasional mop up in between dry spells. Most of the rent money went towards the replacement of ruined appliances from the moisture, and clean ups. He eventually moved out, owing at least two months rent. Susan subsequently dug up the ground around the house and lined the exterior walls, relaying pipes and gutting the finished basement to try and find out where the problem leak was. It never revealed itself but furtively hid in the basement of the house waiting for an appropriate moment to flair up and cripple her.

Phase Five

A nice church lady, referred by the local Minister, was the second tenant of this farmhouse. Susan said she would refinish the basement once she found out the cause of the high humidity levels and occasional flooding, which was evading her up until now. There would be no sense in finishing the basement until this problem could be solved.

The tenant wanted her sister to move into the basement to help pay the rent. This was September. The rent was paid until December. The problem persisted. The basement could not be completed. The rent stopped. Susan got the summons in the mail. Her lovely church-going tenant was suing her for $7,000. She wanted Susan to pay for her move, reimburse her for the new appliances she purchased when she moved in, pay past rent and give her the rent her sister would have paid had she been able to live there.

This is a good example both of the crafty tenant who knows the law and uses it to her full advantage and of the law favoring the tenant, oh, and let's not forget, of the unsuspecting naive landlord standing in the sidelines saying, "What happened?" "What!" "Where am I?"

The creepy crawly revulsion of bad tenants consumed Susan and her past nightmares revisited her with undaunted clarity. History DOES repeat itself. Ha ha. Life is just a bucket of laughs. This was the last straw. Susan spent a fortune on paralegals, faxes, forms, courier services and trips to the courthouse.

Finally, by March, the day in court arrived. The demon in her basement was grasping at her neck as the time approached. Like the hangman's noose failing at the last minute, the paralegal took her aside in the waiting room and revealed she could lose big time. Why not settle out of court and offer a settlement that would cover the tenant's expenses, say, $3,000 and one month's rent? This was accepted and the sweet little smirky church lady left at the end of the month.

Susan was now completely cured of the desire to be a landlord. Paying the mortgage for the farm for the next year out of her own pocket was a pleasure. However, one day she had a look at my lease, and, figuring it covered all the angles, with great trepidation, decided to use it and try, yet again, to find a tenant. (Yeah Charlie Brown!) Even though she found the perfect tenant and yes, to mention, the best lease, she still cringed and bordered on having a panic attack whenever the tenant's number flashed on the display panel of the phone. She just could not handle another wet basement, chimney repair, new roof or cracked wall.

The farm was sold after 6 years of ownership to a local farmer. Susan is a happy and ideal tenant on her farm, now going on 35 years. She is very content to pay the rent promptly and pitch in for repairs on occasion to improve the place. But, ultimately, the problems are not hers. She can walk away from oil spills, floods and leaky roofs.

Susan, at least, has earned the status of being a living legend in her own time, of surviving the horrors of landlordom. Convinced now, that God does not necessarily always reward the good, she likes it just the way it is.

SUMMARY

If you are still with me, you just may have what it takes to be a landlord. After all these horror stories, some of you will, figuratively, hold the book like a dead, poisonous spider between your index finger and thumb, with your pinky up in the air and throw it in the garbage, never again to entertain the idea of renting property to tenants.

But for the rest of you, let's have a review as to how these dire circumstances could be avoided and how prevention is truly the best cure. Here are some pointers to consider, then, to be successful in the rental world and to get the best out of 'Landlordom'.

- Be clear on jobs tenant does: job and payment
- Have good financing to protect your investment
- Keep all receipts and statements
- Budget and keep good records
- Be prepared to keep up with the maintenance and repairs
- File taxes with a good accountant who is familiar with the most recent tax laws pertaining to real estate
- Don't spend good money after bad: If you don't think a tenant will pay rent owing or for damages, absorb your losses, stay out of court and move on.
- Have adequate insurance and keep insurance company up to date
- Get good tenants and research them well; don't rush and rent out of desperation
- Make sure tenants can pay rent, are willing to follow the terms of the lease and will not practice illegal activities
- If you get bad cheques, ask for cash or money order
- Have a good clear lease
- Avoid confrontation
- Set up system to collect rent on time
- Adhere to safety codes
- Make sure infrastructure is sound
- Know the law

Have a comprehensive and clear lease outlining the responsibilities of the landlord and tenant.

Keep rent and payment for jobs, separate. Have them pay the rent and clarify in writing any job they are willing to do and how much you are willing to compensate them. Get a receipt. This avoids any misunderstanding.

Be sure to have a financial plan that ensures money is in the bank to carry you through emergency times and enough to pay for damages or repairs. This lowers the risk of losing your investment because of misfortune.

Keep and maintain good records. Have a good tax accountant and a real estate lawyer on hand.

Maintain your properties. Have a good handy man available.

Be well covered for insurance. Work with your insurance company and let them know of any changes. Know your policy well and be sure you read the small print.

If the tenant owes you money you have the legal right to go after him. However, sometimes just talking with the tenant and saying that you will be obliged to register him as a bad tenant with the credit companies may be enough for him to settle with you before you go any further. Its very stressful to pursue them in court and I have often walked away from it, salvaging whatever I could from the situation and moving forward, being better prepared for the next time.

Some of Susan's nightmarish incidents could have been avoided if she had covered a few bases. Perhaps she could have researched her tenants more thoroughly. Oil tanks do have expiry dates and with a proper building inspection, she could have been reassured that the structure was sound or been alerted to foundation issues and weaknesses.

Never rent out of desperation. Take your time. A bad tenant is worse than no tenant at all. Do your research, call the boss and check the references. Make sure they have a job and can pay the rent. The extra time will pay off in the long run, when you do find the right person.

Limit liabilities by having a safe and secure place with a sound infrastructure. Windows need to be weather proof, doors need to close and locks need to work properly, the heating and plumbing systems have to be fully operational. Get those smoke detectors in and visit the unit once in a while to inspect the safe use of these utilities.

It is also the landlord's responsibility that the units are free of bugs and rodents. On the other hand, if the tenants bring in bed bugs, they have to get rid of them, not the landlord and this is stipulated in the lease. Tenants are obliged to leave the residence clean. Knowing that an inspection is necessary before they leave can help ensure that you will not be left with a mess. This should be in the lease. This is the time when the bonus of $300-$600 will be paid and they will be very motivated to do what it takes to get it.

Avoid confrontation with your tenants. When there is a conflict, deal with it calmly and respectfully. Don't get into a screaming match believing whoever yells the loudest, wins. This is not the case and just makes you look bad, immature and out of control. Keep in mind it is better to work things out than to become enemies and fight it out in court which can be stressful, long and costly.

Also, realize that verbal promises are binding, so be careful what you say.

All to say, know and follow the law. At least be as aware of the law as your tenants are so they can't trap you in the courthouse having to owe them thousands of dollars. If you follow the promises you make in the lease and adhere to Provincial or State guidelines, you will be protecting yourself from potential future problems.

Have all the necessary eviction papers in your files. That way you will have them when you need them and won't be running around at the last minute trying to find the right forms.

Most of what you need to know to start has been covered right here in this manual. Further details can be found on the *Landlord and Tenant Board* site. I have included a couple of other resources that helped me.

Nothing is perfect, but being a landlord can be darned good. Sometimes Jekyll, sometimes Hyde, 'Landordom' is not a place for the feeble, but, if you play your cards right, cross your tees and dot your i's, as they say, chances are you'll be very $ucce$$ful!

I wish you all the best in your new venture.

Christine Dorothy

RESOURCES

Landlord and Tenant Board www.ltb.gov.on.ca

Residential Tenancy Act (RTA)
Ontario Tenants' and Landlords Rights and Responsibilities. http://www.ontariotenants.ca

TD Credit Application, www.secure.tdcanadatrust.com/apply/credit/apply

Credit Companies Equifax, www.equifax.com, Trans Union, www.tuc.com

FORMS

Rent

 Landlord
and
Tenant
Board

Form N4 - Checklist
Notice to End a Tenancy Early for Non-payment of Rent

Before you serve the attached notice to your tenant(s), make sure you can answer **YES** to each of the following questions. If not, your notice may be invalid. If you file an application to the Landlord and Tenant Board based on an invalid notice, your application may be dismissed and you will have to start over.

☐   **Did you fill in the correct termination date?**
If your tenant pays rent by the **month** or **year**, you must give **at least 14 days** notice. If your tenant pays rent by the **day** or **week**, you must give **at least 7 days** notice.

When counting the days, do not include the date you are giving the notice to the tenant. For example, if you give the notice to the tenant by hand on March 3rd, the first day of the 14-day notice period is March 4th; in this example, the earliest termination date would be March 17th. **If you are giving the notice to the tenant by mail or courier, you have to add extra days in calculating the termination date.** Read the Instructions to this form to see how much time you have to add.

☐   **Did you name each tenant who lives in the rental unit?**
If there is more than one tenant living in the rental unit, fill in the names of all the tenants.

☐   **Did you fill in the complete address of the rental unit?**
Be sure that you have provided the full address - including the correct unit number and postal code.

☐   **Did you check your math?**
Make sure you've correctly calculated the amount you believe the tenant owes. Check the calculations in the table on page 2 to be sure the Total Rent Owing is correct. Then check that this amount matches the amount you put in the box on page 1.

☐   **Did you include only rent amounts?**
This form is only for non-payment of **rent**. Rent includes the basic rent for the rental unit, plus any amount the tenant pays you separately for services (such as parking or cable). If the tenant is paying all or a portion of a utility bill directly to the utility company or indirectly through the landlord, this is not considered rent. See the Instructions for more information.

You should **not** use this form to tell the tenant they have failed to pay amounts other than rent (such as the last month's rent deposit or an NSF cheque charge).

☐   **Did you sign and date the notice?**

You should remove this checklist before you give the tenant the notice.

Notice To End a Tenancy Early For Non-payment of Rent

Form N4

To: (Tenant's name)

From: (Landlord's name)

This is a legal notice that could lead to you being evicted from your home.

Address of the Rental Unit

Street Number   Street Name

Street Type (e.g. Street, Avenue, Road)   Direction (e.g. East)   Unit/Apt./Suite

Municipality (city, town, etc.)   Province   O N   Postal Code

This information is from your landlord:

I am giving you this notice because I believe you owe me $ [ ] , [ ] . [ ] in rent.

See the table on the next page for the details about how I calculated this amount.

I can apply to the Landlord and Tenant Board to have you evicted if you do not:

- **pay this amount*** by [ ] / [ ] / [ ]   This date is called the termination date.
  dd   mm   yyyy

or

- **move out by the termination date**

* If another rent payment comes due on or before the date you make the above payment to your landlord, you must also pay this extra amount.

WHAT YOU NEED TO KNOW

The following information is provided by the Landlord and Tenant Board

The termination date
The date that the landlord gives you in this notice to pay or move out must be at least:
- 14 days after the landlord gives you the notice, if you rent by the month or year, or
- 7 days after the landlord gives you the notice, if you rent by the day or week.

What if you agree with the notice
If you agree that you owe the amount that the landlord is claiming, you should pay this amount by the termination date in this notice. If you do so, this notice becomes void and the landlord cannot apply to the Board to evict you. If you do not pay the amount owing, and the landlord applies to the Board to evict you, you will likely have to pay the landlord's filing fee of $170.00, plus what you owe.

If you move out by the date in this notice, your tenancy will end on the termination date. However, you may still owe money to your landlord. Your landlord will not be able to apply to the Board but they may still take you to Court for this money.

What if you disagree with the notice
If you disagree with what the landlord has put in this notice, you do not have to move out. You could talk to your landlord. You may also want to get legal advice. If you cannot work things out, and the landlord applies to the Board, you will be able to go to a hearing and explain why you disagree.

10101

84   CHRISTINE DOROTHY

How you will know if the landlord applies to the Board	The earliest date that the landlord can apply to the Board is the day after the termination date in this notice. If the landlord does apply, the Board will schedule a hearing and send you a letter. The landlord must also give you a copy of the Notice of Hearing and the application.
What you can do if the landlord applies to the Board	• Get legal advice immediately; you may be eligible for legal aid services. • Talk to your landlord about working out a payment plan. • Go to the hearing where you can respond to your landlord's claims; in most cases, before the hearing starts you can also talk to a Board mediator about mediating a payment plan.
How to get more information	For more information about this notice or about your rights, you can contact the Landlord and Tenant Board. You can reach the Board by phone at **416-645-8080** or toll-free at **1-888-332-3234**. You can also visit the Board's website at **www.LTB.gov.on.ca**.

This table is completed by the landlord to show how they calculated the total amount of rent claimed on page 1:

Rent Period		Rent Charged $	Rent Paid $	Rent Owing $
From: (dd/mm/yyyy)	To: (dd/mm/yyyy)			
/ /	/ /			
/ /	/ /			
/ /	/ /			
			Total Rent Owing $	

Signature   ☐ Landlord ☐ Agent

Signature	Date (dd/mm/yyyy)

First Name

Last Name

Company Name (if applicable)

Mailing Address

Unit/Apt./Suite | Municipality (city, town, etc.) | Province

Postal Code | Phone Number ( ) | Fax Number ( )

E-mail Address

10101

Page 2 of 2

Form L1 Application to Evict a Tenant for Non-Payment of Rent and to Collect Rent the Tenant owes

Landlord
and
Tenant Board

Form L1

Application to Evict a Tenant for Non-Payment of Rent and to Collect Rent the Tenant Owes

Instructions

April 6, 2009

SECTION A   When to use this application

If you have given your tenant an N4 notice of termination (for non-payment of rent) and the tenant has not paid the rent they owe or has not moved out, you can file this application with the Landlord and Tenant Board (the Board), if you want to:

- end the tenancy and evict the tenant, and
- collect the money the tenant owes you up to the date they move out of the rental unit

If the tenant made a payment by cheque that was returned to you due to non-sufficient funds (NSF) and the tenant has not paid you back for the charges related to that, you may include these amounts in your application.

You cannot file this application until the day **after** the termination date you put on the N4 notice.

In order for you to file this application, the tenant must still be living in the rental unit. If the tenant has already moved out, you cannot apply to the Board but you can apply to court for the money the tenant owes you.

If you do not want to evict your tenant, but you want to get an order from the Board so that you can collect the rent the tenant owes you, you can complete the *Application to collect rent the tenant owes* (Form L9) and file it with the Board. In order for you to file the L9 application, however, the tenant must still be living in the rental unit. You should also be aware that if the Board issues an order on an L9 application and the tenant still does not pay, you cannot use that order to evict the tenant.

SECTION B   How to complete this application

You must be sure that your application meets the requirements of the *Residential Tenancies Act* (the Act). Read the following instructions and complete the application form carefully.

The information you fill in on the form will be read electronically; therefore it is very important that you follow these instructions carefully:

- Print in **capital letters** and do not touch the edges of the boxes.
- If there are more boxes in a line than you need, start from the left and leave the extra boxes blank.
- Do not fill in boxes that do not apply to you (for example, if you do not have a fax number, do not fill in boxes in the space marked "Fax Number").

- If the instructions tell you to shade a box (for example, boxes marked "Yes" or "No"), shade the box completely.

It is the applicant's responsibility to ensure that their application is correct and complete. Staff of the Landlord and Tenant Board will check applications for completeness; however, the Board Member who will make a decision on the application will ultimately determine whether or not it meets the requirements of the legislation. Where it does not, the application may be dismissed.

On Page 1 of the Application form:

DO NOT FILL IN the amount you believe the tenant owes you until you have completed page 4 of the application. Once you calculate the total amount owing on page 4, you will copy that amount to page 1. This is the total amount that the tenant owes you on the date that you file your application with the Board.

The date you fill in on page 1 is the date you file the application with the Board.

On Page 3 of the Application form:

Part 1: Rental unit covered by this application:

Fill in the complete address of the rental unit, including the unit number and the postal code.

Example:
If the address is: #208 at 1120 Mayfield Road North, London, this is how Part 1 of the application should be completed:

Street Number	Street Name
1 1 2 0	M A Y F I E L D

Street Type (e.g. Street, Avenue, Road)	Direction (e.g. East)	Unit/Apt./Suite
R O A D	N O R T H	2 0 8

Municipality (city, town, etc.)	Province	Postal Code
L O N D O N	O N	N 6 3 2 M 1

If the street name includes a direction that will not fit in the five spaces provided (such as Northeast) use the following abbreviations: NE for Northeast, NW for Northwest, SE for Southeast, SW for Southwest.

Related Applications:
If any other applications have been filed with the Landlord and Tenant Board that relate to the same rental unit, fill in the file numbers of those applications.

Part 2: Tenant names and addresses:

To: Fill in the tenant's name. If two tenants live in the rental unit, fill in both their names. If more than two tenants live in the rental unit, first complete Part 1 of the application form and then provide the names, addresses and telephone numbers of any additional tenants on the "Schedule of Parties" form which is available from the Board.

Where there is a subtenant or assignee, you should also name these people in the application; however, you do not need to name other occupants, such as children or guests of the tenant.

Fill in the tenant's mailing address **only** if it is different from the address of the rental unit. Provide the tenant's daytime and evening telephone numbers and a fax number and e-mail address, if you know them.

Part 3: Reason for this application:

Shade the appropriate box or boxes to indicate what you are applying for.

Shade either the **Yes** or **No** box to answer the question, "Is the tenant still in possession of the rental unit on the date this application is filed with the Board?" A landlord may only file this application if the tenant is still in possession of the rental unit.

Shade the appropriate box to indicate whether the tenant pays rent by the **Week**, **Month** or **Other**. If you choose Other, write in the frequency of rent payments (for example, bi-weekly) in the space provided.

Information about the rent deposit:
The Board will subtract any rent deposit and interest you owe the tenant from the amount of rent the tenant owes you. If you collected a rent deposit from the tenant, answer the questions about the deposit. If you did not collect a deposit, leave these boxes blank.

On Page 4 of the Application form:

Part 4: Details of the Landlord's claim:

Section 1. Rent Owing
Complete the Rent Owing table to show how you calculated the amount of rent [1] the tenant owes you. The example below will help you complete the table.

---

[1] **Rent** includes the basic rent for the rental unit, plus any amount the tenant pays you separately for services (such as parking or cable). If the tenant is responsible for paying all or a portion of a utility bill (such as hydro) directly to the utility company or indirectly through the landlord, this is not considered rent. However, if the tenant is required to pay a flat rate to the landlord each month for a utility, this would meet the definition of rent.

If the tenant owes more than they did when you served them the Form N4 Notice of Termination, include all the rent owing up to the date you file the application.

If the tenant owes you rent for more than three rental periods, you can combine two or more rental periods in the first or second row of the table. However, in the last row of the table that you complete, you must show the rent charged, rent paid and rent owing for the last rent period for which the tenant owes rent. The Board needs this information in order to calculate the amount of daily compensation the tenant owes for each day they remain in the unit without paying after the termination date.

If you believe that your own ledger or account summary is more clear you can attach a sheet that shows the details but you must still provide a summary in the table.

Example:

The tenancy agreement between Bruce Campanolo, the landlord, and Sophia Maxwell, the tenant, requires Sophia to pay $900 on the first of each month. On January 1st, 2007 she paid only $850 and on February 1st, she did not pay any rent. On February 3rd, Bruce gave Sophia a Notice to End the Tenancy Early for Non-payment of Rent. The notice set out that she owed $950 and that she had until February 17th to pay or move. Sophie did not pay or move by February 17th, so on February 18th Bruce filed this application with the Board. This is how he filled out the rent owing table:

I have calculated the amount of rent the tenant owes me as follows:

Rent Period From: (dd/mm/yyyy)	To: (dd/mm/yyyy)	Rent Charged $	Rent Paid $	Rent Owing $
01/01/2007	31/01/2007	900.00	850.00	50.00
01/02/2007	28/02/2007	900.00	0.00	900.00
/ /	/ /	.	.	.
			Total Rent Owing $	950.00

Section 2. NSF Cheque Charges

If the tenant made a payment by cheque that was returned to you due to non-sufficient funds (NSF), and the tenant has not paid you back for the charges related to the NSF cheque, you may include these amounts in your application.

Complete the table to show how you calculated the amount the tenant owes you. For each NSF cheque the tenant gave you, complete one row of the table. Fill in the amount and date of the cheque, the date your financial institution charged you for the NSF cheque, the amount of the bank charge for the NSF cheque, and the amount of your related administration charges.

The "Bank charge for NSF cheque" is the actual amount your financial institution charged you. "Administration charges" is not defined in the Act or the regulations, but may include your personal or corporate costs related to the handling of NSF rent cheques. For example, when a cheque "bounces", you may have to do additional accounting, notify the tenant of the NSF cheque, make another request for payment and possibly receive another payment. The maximum administration charge for an NSF cheque allowed by the Act is $20 per cheque.

Example:

Sophia Maxwell, the tenant, gave Bruce Campanolo, the landlord, a cheque for $900.00, dated February 1st for February's rent, but the cheque was returned NSF. As a result, the bank charged Bruce an NSF fee of $5; the fee appeared on his bank statement on February 20th. Bruce also had costs related to the handling of the NSF cheque. Bruce served Sophia with a Notice to End the Tenancy Early for Non-payment of Rent. Sophia did not pay the rent by the termination date in the notice so Bruce applied to terminate the tenancy.

Bruce filled out the table as shown below to show how he calculated the amount owing for the NSF related charges:

I have calculated the amount of NSF cheque charges and related administration charges the tenant owes me as follows:

Cheque Amount $	Date of Cheque dd/mm/yyyy	Date NSF Charge Incurred dd/mm/yyyy	Bank Charge for NSF Cheque $	Landlord's Administration Charge $	Total Charge $
900.00	01/02/2007	20/02/2007	5.00	20.00	25.00
.	/ /	/ /	.	.	.
.	/ /	/ /	.	.	.
.	/ /	/ /	.	.	.
.	/ /	/ /	.	.	.

Total NSF Related Charges Owing $ 25.00

Part 5: Total amount owing:

Transfer the Total Rent Owing amount from Section 1 of Part 4 to this part of the form.

Transfer the Total NSF Cheque Charges from Section 2 of Part 4 to this part of the form.

Calculate the Total Amount Owing. Then, transfer this amount to the box on Page 1. The date you fill in on page 1 is the date you file the application with the Board.

On Page 5 of the Application form:

Part 6: Landlord's name and address:

Fill in the landlord's name and address, and shade the appropriate box to show whether the landlord is male, female or a company. If the landlord is a company, fill in the name of the company under "First Name". Include both daytime and evening telephone numbers and a fax number and e-mail address, if you have them.

If there is more than one landlord, first complete Part 1 with information about one of the landlords, then provide the names, addresses and telephone numbers of the additional landlords on the "Schedule of Parties" form which is available from the Board.

If the person who signs the application form is an agent for the landlord or an officer of a corporation, provide that person's name, the company name (if applicable), mailing address, telephone, fax number and e-mail address.

On Page 6 of the Application form:

Part 7: Signature:

If you are the landlord, shade the box marked "Landlord". Then, sign the application form and fill in the date.

If you are an agent for the landlord, shade the box marked "Agent". Then, sign the application form and fill in the date.

L1 Payment and Scheduling Information Form

Complete this form to provide the Board with the information required to process your application. The fee for this application is $170.00. Your application will not be accepted if you do not pay the application fee at the time you file the application.

If you owe money to the Board as a result of failing to pay a fee or any fine or costs set out in an order, your application may be refused or discontinued.

Part 1:   Application Fee

Shade the appropriate box to show whether you are paying by cash, debit card, money order, certified cheque, Visa, MasterCard or American Express. You cannot pay by cash or debit card if you are filing your application by fax or mail. If you are paying by credit card, include the cardholder's name and signature, the card number and expiry date.

The information you fill in on this part of the form is confidential. It will be used to process your application, but will not be placed on the application file.

Part 2: Information Required to Schedule the Hearing

How do you want the Board to give you the application package?

If you file your application in person at a Board office, in most cases the Board will be able to schedule a hearing and prepare the application package (see Section D below) while you wait. However, if you mail or fax your application, you must tell the Board whether you would like to pick up the application package at a Board or ServiceOntario office, or have it mailed to you or faxed to you. Shade the appropriate box to show how you want to receive the application package.

If you want to pick up the application package at a Board or ServiceOntario office, also indicate what day and at what office you would like to pick it up. If you are mailing your application to the Board, the earliest day you can ask to pick up the package is six days after you mail it. If you are faxing your application, the earliest day you can ask to pick up the package is the day after you fax it. In either case, call the Board before picking up the package to make sure it is ready.

When will you give the application package to the tenant?

Shade the appropriate box to indicate whether you will give the tenant the application package (the tenant's copy of the Notice of Hearing and the application) on the date you receive it from the Board or on a different date. If you intend to give the application package to the tenant on a different date, fill in the date in the space provided. The Board must know this date in order to schedule the hearing.

How will you give the application package to the tenant?

The Board also needs to know how you plan to give the application package to the tenant. Shade the appropriate box to indicate whether you will be mailing the package, sending it by courier or giving it some other way.

Part 3: Interpretation Services Required

Shade the appropriate box or boxes to indicate whether you require French language services or Sign language services.

The Board will only provide French language services if you live in an area of the Province designated for French language services or if the rental unit or complex that is covered by the application is in an area designated for French language services. If you are not sure if you live in a designated area, you can contact the Board for more information.

If you require sign language services, the Board will arrange for an interpreter to attend the hearing.

SECTION C How and where to file this application

To file this application, you need:

- the completed application form (including the L1 Payment and Scheduling form)
- the filing fee ($170.00)
- a copy of the Form N4 Notice to End the Tenancy Early for Non-payment of Rent you gave the tenant
- a Certificate of Service showing how and when you gave the tenant the Form N4

Your application will be refused if any of the items listed is missing.

To file this application, you can:

1. **Bring it** to the nearest Board office.

   If you file your application in person, you can pay the filing fee by cash, certified cheque, money order, Visa, American Express or MasterCard. You can also pay by debit card at most locations.

2. **Fax it** to the Regional Board office in your area.

   If you fax your application, you must pay the filing fee by Visa, American Express or MasterCard.

3. **Mail it** to the Regional Board office in your area.

   If you mail your application, you can pay the filing fee by certified cheque, money order, Visa, American Express or MasterCard.

Certified cheques and money orders must be made payable to the Minister of Finance.

SECTION D What the Board will do after you file this application

Once you have filed the application and paid the application fee, the Board will schedule a hearing. If you apply in person, the Board will normally schedule the hearing while you wait. Generally, the Board will schedule an oral hearing. An oral hearing is a meeting between the landlord and the tenant before an adjudicator. However, in some circumstances the Board may decide it is appropriate to have a written, telephone or video conference hearing instead.

The Board will give you an application package that consists of the following documents:

- a copy of the application and a Notice of Hearing to keep for yourself
- a blank Certificate of Service form (see Section E below for instructions on how to fill out this form)
- a copy of the application and the Notice of Hearing for the tenant
- instructions for giving the application and the Notice of Hearing to the tenant.

The Board will also give you:

- a blank Payment Agreement form that you and your tenant can use to settle your application if you come to an agreement before the hearing
- a brochure called, *Important Information about your Hearing.*

SECTION E   What you have to do after you file this application

You must give the tenant a copy of the application and a copy of the Notice of Hearing at least **ten days** before the hearing. There are many ways that you can give this notice to your tenant. Refer to the Instructions that are included in the application package the Board will give you when you file your application.

You must file a Certificate of Service with the Board showing when and how you gave a copy of the application and the Notice of Hearing to the tenant. You must file the certificate within **five days** after you served these documents. The Certificate of Service form is included in the package the Board will give you when you file your application.

You should come to the hearing prepared to support your application. If there are any documents or other information that you will be relying on, you should bring them to the hearing. You should bring extra copies for the Board and the tenant. For example, you should bring evidence of the rent charged and the rent paid during the period(s) for which the tenant is in arrears of rent. You should also bring any witnesses you may need to prove your claim. If you need to summon a witness, you can obtain a *Request for the Board to Issue a Summons* form from your local Board office or the Board's website at www.LTB.gov.on.ca.

You should also come prepared for any issues the tenant might raise at the hearing. At a hearing for an application to end a tenancy early based on non-payment of rent, the tenant is allowed to raise any issue they could raise on any of the Board's tenant applications. For example, a tenant could raise such issues as maintenance or illegal rent. To avoid any delay in the hearing, you should consider whether or not it is likely that your tenant will do this, and be prepared to discuss the issues. For more information about this, you may want to read the Board's brochure called, *Issues a Tenant Can Raise at a Hearing about a Landlord's Application for Non-payment of Rent* (Form L1 or L9).

Who to contact if you have any questions

If you need more information or have any questions, you can call the Landlord and Tenant Board at 416-645-8080 or toll-free at 1-888-332-3234. Or, you can visit the Board's website at www.LTB.gov.on.ca

Form L9 Application to Collect Rent the Tenant Owes

Landlord
and
Tenant Board

Form L9

Application to Collect Rent the Tenant Owes

Instructions

June 19, 2009

SECTION A When to use this application

If your tenant has not paid the rent they owe, you can file this application with the Landlord and Tenant Board (the Board) to get an order that requires the tenant to pay what they owe. If the tenant made a payment by cheque that was returned to you due to non-sufficient funds (NSF) and the tenant has not paid you back for the charges related to that, you may include these amounts in your application.

In order for you to file this application, the tenant must still be living in the rental unit. If the tenant has already moved out, you cannot apply to the Board but you can apply to court for the money the tenant owes you.

If you want to apply to the Board to have your tenant evicted for non-payment of rent, the application you have to file is the *Application to evict a tenant for non-payment of rent and to collect rent the tenant owes* (Form L1). However, before you can file the L1 application, you will first have to give the tenant a *Notice to End the Tenancy for Non-payment of Rent* (Form N4). For more information about that process, read the Board's information brochures: *If a tenant doesn't pay rent* and *How a Landlord can End a Tenancy*.

SECTION B How to complete this application

You must be sure that your application meets the requirements of the *Residential Tenancies Act* (the Act). Read the following instructions and complete the application form carefully.

The information you fill in on the form will be read electronically; therefore it is very important that you follow these instructions carefully:

- Print in **capital letters** and do not touch the edges of the boxes.
- If there are more boxes in a line than you need, start from the left and leave the extra boxes blank.
- Do not fill in boxes that do not apply to you (for example, if you do not have a fax number, do not fill in boxes in the space marked "Fax Number").
- If the instructions tell you to shade a box (for example, boxes marked "Yes" or "No"), shade the box completely.

It is the applicant's responsibility to ensure that their application is correct and complete. Staff of the Landlord and Tenant Board will check applications for completeness; however, the Board Member who will make a decision on the application will ultimately determine whether or not it meets the requirements of the legislation. Where it does not, the application may be dismissed.

On Page 1 of the Application form:

Do not fill in the amount you believe the tenant owes you until you have completed page 4 of the application. Once you calculate the total amount owing on page 4, you will copy that amount to page 1. This is the total amount that the tenant owes you on the date that you file your application with the Board.

The date you fill in on page 1 is the date you file the application with the Board.

On Page 3 of the Application form:

Part 1: Rental unit covered by this application:

Fill in the complete address of the rental unit, including the unit number and the postal code.

Example:
If the address is: #208 at 1120 Mayfield Road North, London, this is how Part 1 of the application should be completed:

Street Number	Street Name					
1 1 2 0	M A Y F I E L D					
Street Type (e.g. Street, Avenue, Road)	Direction (e.g. East)	Unit/Apt./Suite				
R O A D	N O R T H	2 0 8				
Municipality (city, town, etc.)	Province	Postal Code				
L O N D O N	O N	N 6 J 2 M 1				

If the street name includes a direction that will not fit in the five spaces provided (such as Northeast) use the following abbreviations: NE for Northeast, NW for Northwest, SE for Southeast, SW for Southwest.

Related Applications:
If any other applications have been filed with the Landlord and Tenant Board that relate to the same rental unit, fill in the file numbers of those applications.

Part 2: Tenant names and addresses:

To: Fill in the tenant's name. If two tenants live in the rental unit, fill in both their names. If more than two tenants live in the rental unit, first complete Part 1 of the application form and then provide the names, addresses and telephone numbers of any additional tenants on the "Schedule of Parties" form which is available from the Board.

Where there is a subtenant or assignee, you should also name these people in the application; however, other occupants, such as children or guests of the tenant, do not need to be named.

Fill in the tenant's mailing address only if it is different from the address of the rental unit. Provide the tenant's daytime and evening telephone numbers and a fax number and e-mail address, if you know them.

Part 3: Reason for this application:

Shade the appropriate box or boxes to indicate what you are applying for.

Shade either the **Yes** or **No** box to answer the question, "Is the tenant still in possession of the rental unit on the date this application is filed with the Board?" A landlord may only file this application if the tenant is still in possession of the rental unit.

Shade the appropriate box to indicate whether the tenancy is **Weekly, Monthly** or **Other**. If you choose Other, write in the type of tenancy (for example, bi-weekly) in the space provided.

On Page 4 of the Application form:

Part 4: Details of the Landlord's claim:

Section 1. Rent Owing

Complete the Rent Owing table to show how you calculated the amount of rent [1] the tenant owes you. The example below will help you complete the table.

If the tenant owes you rent for more than three rental periods, you can combine two or more rental periods in the first or second row of the table. However, in the last row of the table that you complete, you must show the rent charged, rent paid and rent owing for the last rent period for which the tenant owes rent.

If you believe that your own ledger or account summary is more clear you can attach a sheet that shows the details but, you must still provide a summary in the table.

Example:

The tenancy agreement between Bruce Campanolo, the landlord, and Sophia Maxwell, the tenant, requires Sophia to pay $900 on the first of each month. On January 1st, 2007 she paid only $850 and on February 1st, she did not pay any rent. On February 3rd, Bruce filed this application with the Board. This is how he filled out the rent owing table:

---

[1] **Rent** includes the basic rent for the rental unit, plus any amount the tenant pays you separately for services (such as parking or cable). If the tenant is responsible for paying all or a portion of a utility bill (such as hydro) directly to the utility company or indirectly through the landlord, this is not considered rent. However, if the tenant is required to pay a flat rate to the landlord each month for a utility, this would meet the definition of rent.

I have calculated the amount of rent the tenant owes me as follows:

Rent Period		Rent Charged $	Rent Paid $	Rent Owing $
From: (dd/mm/yyyy)	To: (dd/mm/yyyy)			
01/01/2007	31/01/2007	900.00	850.00	50.00
01/02/2007	28/02/2007	900.00	0.00	900.00
/ /	/ /	.	.	.
		Total Rent Owing $		950.00

Section 2. NSF Cheque Charges

If the tenant made a payment by cheque that was returned to you due to non-sufficient funds (NSF), and the tenant has not paid you back for the charges related to the NSF cheque, you may include these amounts in your application.

Complete the table to show how you calculated the amount the tenant owes you. For each NSF cheque the tenant gave you, complete one row of the table. Fill in the amount and date of the cheque, the date your financial institution charged you for the NSF cheque, the amount of the bank charge for the NSF cheque, and the amount of your related administration charges.

The "Bank charge for NSF cheque" is the actual amount your financial institution charged you. "Administration charges" is not defined in the Act or the regulations, but may include your personal or corporate costs related to the handling of NSF rent cheques. For example, when a cheque "bounces", you may have to do additional accounting, notify the tenant of the NSF cheque, make another request for payment and possibly receive another payment. The maximum administration charge for an NSF cheque allowed by the RTA is $20 per cheque.

Example:

Sophia Maxwell, the tenant, gave Bruce Campanolo, the landlord, a cheque for $900.00, dated February 1st for February's rent, but the cheque was returned NSF. As a result, the bank charged Bruce an NSF fee of $5; the fee appeared on his bank statement on February 20th. Bruce also had costs related to the handling of the NSF cheque.

Bruce filled out the table as shown below to show how he calculated the amount owing for the NSF related charges:

I have calculated the amount of NSF cheque charges and related administration charges the tenant owes me as follows:

Cheque Amount $	Date of Cheque dd/mm/yyyy	Date NSF Charge Incurred dd/mm/yyyy	Bank Charge for NSF Cheque $	Landlord's Administration Charge $	Total Charge $
900.00	01/02/2007	20/02/2007	5.00	20.00	25.00
.	/ /	/ /	.	.	.
.	/ /	/ /	.	.	.
.	/ /	/ /	.	.	.
.	/ /	/ /	.	.	.

Total NSF Related Charges Owing $ 25.00

Part 5: Total amount owing:

Transfer the Total Rent Owing amount from Section 1 of Part 4 to this part of the form.

Transfer the Total NSF Cheque Charges from Section 2 of Part 4 to this part of the form.

Calculate the Total Amount Owing. Then, transfer this amount to the box on Page 1. The date you fill in on page 1 is the date you file the application with the Board.

On Page 5 of the Application form:

Part 6: Landlord's name and address:

Fill in the landlord's name and address, and shade the appropriate box to show whether the landlord is male, female or a company. If the landlord is a company, fill in the name of the company under "First Name". Include both daytime and evening telephone numbers and a fax number and e-mail address, if you have them.

If there is more than one landlord, first complete Part 1 with information about one of the landlords, then provide the names, addresses and telephone numbers of the additional landlords on the "Schedule of Parties" form which is available from the Board.

If the person who signs the application form is an agent for the landlord or an officer of a corporation, provide that person's name, the company name (if applicable), mailing address, telephone, fax number and e-mail address.

On Page 6 of the Application form:

Part 7: Signature:

If you are the landlord, shade the box marked "Landlord". Then, sign the application form and fill in the date.

If you are an agent for the landlord, shade the box marked "Agent". Then, sign the application form and fill in the date.

L9 Payment and Scheduling Information Form

Complete this form to provide the Board with the information required to process your application. The fee for this application is $170.00. Your application will not be accepted if you do not pay the application fee at the time you file the application.

If you owe money to the Board as a result of failing to pay a fee or any fine or costs set out in an order, your application may be refused or discontinued.

Part 1:   Application Fee

Shade the appropriate box to show whether you are paying by cash, debit card, money order, certified cheque, Visa, MasterCard or American Express. You cannot pay by cash or debit card if you are filing your application by fax or mail. If you are paying by credit card, include the cardholder's name and signature, the card number and expiry date.

The information you fill in on this part of the form is confidential. It will be used to process your application, but will not be placed on the application file.

Part 2:   Information Required to Schedule the Hearing

How do you want the Board to give you the application package?

If you file your application in person at a Board office, in most cases the Board will be able to schedule a hearing and prepare the application package while you wait. However, if you mail or fax your application, you must tell the Board whether you would like to pick up the application package at a Board or ServiceOntario office, or have it mailed to you or faxed to you. Shade the appropriate box to show how you want to receive the application package.

If you want to pick up the application package at a Board or ServiceOntario office, also indicate what day and at what office you would like to pick it up. If you are mailing your application to the Board, the earliest day you can ask to pick up the package is six days after you mail it. If you are faxing your application, the earliest day you can ask to pick up the package is the day after you fax it. In either case, call the Board before picking up the package to make sure it is ready.

When will you give the application package to the tenant?

Shade the appropriate box to indicate whether you will give the tenant the application package (the tenant's copy of the Notice of Hearing and the application) on the date you receive it from the Board or on a different date. If you intend to give the application package to the tenant on a different date, fill in the date in the space provided. The Board must know this date in order to schedule the hearing.

How will you give the application package to the tenant?

The Board also needs to know how you plan to give the application package to the tenant. Shade the appropriate box to indicate whether you will be mailing the package, sending it by courier or giving it some other way.

Part 3:　Interpretation Services Required

Shade the appropriate box or boxes to indicate whether you require French language services or Sign language services.

The Board will only provide French language services if you live in an area of the Province designated for French language services or if the rental unit or complex that is covered by the application is in an area designated for French language services. If you are not sure if you live in a designated area, you can contact the Board for more information.

If you require sign language services, the Board will arrange for an interpreter to attend the hearing.

 How and where to file this application

To file this application, you need:

- the completed application form (including the L9 Payment and Scheduling form), and

- the filing fee ($170.00)

To file this application, you can:

1. **Bring it** to the nearest Board office.

   If you file your application in person, you can pay the filing fee by cash, certified cheque, money order, Visa, American Express or MasterCard. You can also pay by debit card at most locations.

2. **Fax it** to the Regional Board office in your area.

    If you fax your application, you must pay the filing fee by Visa, American Express or MasterCard.

3. **Mail it** to the Regional Board office in your area.

    If you mail your application, you can pay the filing fee by certified cheque, money order, Visa, American Express or MasterCard.

SECTION D — What the Board will do after you file this application

Once you have filed the application and paid the application fee, the Board will schedule a hearing. If you apply in person, the Board will normally schedule the hearing while you wait. Generally, the Board will schedule an oral hearing. An oral hearing is a meeting between the landlord and the tenant before an adjudicator. However, in some circumstances the Board may decide it is appropriate to have a written, telephone or video conference hearing instead.

The Board will give you an application package that consists of the following documents:

- a copy of the application and a Notice of Hearing to keep for yourself
- a blank Certificate of Service form (see Section E below for instructions)
- a copy of the application and the Notice of Hearing for the tenant
- instructions for giving the application and the Notice of Hearing to the tenant.

The Board will also give you:

- a blank Payment Agreement form that you and your tenant can use to settle your application if you come to an agreement before the hearing
- a brochure called, *Important Information about your Hearing.*

SECTION E — What you have to do after you file this application

You must give the tenant a copy of the application and a copy of the Notice of Hearing at least **ten days** before the hearing. There are many ways that you can give this notice to your tenant. Refer to the Instructions that are included in the application package the Board will give you when you file your application.

You must file a Certificate of Service with the Board showing when and how you gave a copy of the application and the Notice of Hearing to the tenant. You must file the certificate within **five days** after you served these documents. The Certificate of Service form is included in the package the Board will give you when you file your application.

You should come to the hearing prepared to support your application. If there are any documents or other information that you will be relying on, you should bring them to the hearing. You should bring extra copies for the Board and the tenant. For example, you should bring evidence of the rent charged and the rent paid during the period(s) for which the tenant is in arrears of rent. You should also bring any witnesses you may need to prove your claim. If you need to summon a witness, you can obtain a "Request for the Board to Issue a Summons" form from your local Board office or the Board's website at www.LTB.gov.on.ca.

You should also come prepared for any issues the tenant might raise at the hearing. The Act allows a tenant to raise any issue they could raise on any of the Board's tenant applications, at a hearing on this type of landlord application. For example, a tenant could raise such issues as maintenance or illegal rent. To avoid any delay in the hearing, you should consider whether or not it is likely that your tenant will do this, and be prepared to discuss the issues. For more information about this, you may want to read the Board's brochure called, *Issues a Tenant Can Raise at a Hearing about a Landlord's Application for Non-payment of Rent (Form L1 or L9)*.

 Who to contact if you have any questions

If you need more information or have any questions, you can call the Landlord and Tenant Board at 416-645-8080 or toll-free at 1-888-332-3234. Or, you can visit the Board's website at www.LTB.gov.on.ca.

Form N1 Notice of Rent Increase

Notice of Rent Increase
Form N1

Read the instructions carefully before completing this form.

To: (Tenant's name and address)	From: (Landlord's name and address)

Address of the Rental Unit:

Your New Rent

On _____ , your rent will increase to $ _____
(day/month/year)

per _____ .
(month, week, etc.)

This rent includes the basic rent for your rental unit, plus any amount you pay separately to your landlord for services.

Explanation of the Rent Increase

This is a rent increase of. $ _____ per _____ or _____ %.
(month, week, etc.)

Shade one of the following:

☐ This rent increase is less than or equal to the rent increase guideline and does not need approval by an order under the *Residential Tenancies Act*.

OR

☐ This rent increase is more than the rent increase guideline, but:

1. ☐ The rent increase has been approved by an order under the *Tenant Protection Act* or the *Residential Tenancies Act*.

2. ☐ The rent increase must be approved by an order under the *Tenant Protection Act* or the *Residential Tenancies Act*. I have applied to the Tribunal or the Board for a Rent Increase Above the Guideline.

Important Information About the Law

1. The landlord must give the tenant this notice at least 90 days before the date of the rent increase. A landlord may increase the rent if at least 12 months have passed since the last rent increase or since a new tenant moved into the rental unit. No Notice of Rent Increase is required where the landlord and tenant have signed an Agreement to Increase the Rent Above the Guideline (Form N10)

2. A tenant does not have to sign a new lease when a fixed term tenancy ends. If the tenant decides not to sign a new lease, the tenant does not have to move, but the tenancy becomes "month-to-month".

   If a tenant plans to move, the tenant must notify the landlord on Form N9 (Tenant's Notice to Terminate the Tenancy) at least 60 days before the lease expires if the tenant has a fixed term of tenancy or 60 days before the end of a monthly or yearly rental period. The tenant must notify the landlord on Form N9 at least 28 days before the end of a weekly rental period

3. If the rent increase needs approval by an order under the *Tenant Protection Act* or the *Residential Tenancies Act*, the tenant is not required to pay more than the guideline increase until the order is issued. If the tenant only pays the guideline increase, the tenant may owe the landlord once the order is issued.

4. If you have any questions about the law related to rent increases and how it applies to this notice, you can contact the Landlord and Tenant Board at **416-645-8080** or toll-free at **1-888-332-3234**. Or, you may also visit the Board's website at **www.LTB.gov.on.ca** for further information.

Signature   ☐ Landlord   ☐ Agent

Name of Person Signing	Phone Number
Signature	Date

Agent Information (if applicable)

Name		Company Name (if applicable)	
Mailing Address			Phone Number
Municipality (city, town, etc.)	Province	Postal Code	Fax Number

www.ingramcontent.com/pod-product-compliance
Lightning Source LLC
Chambersburg PA
CBHW022104170526
45157CB00004B/1470